The New Gray's Wild Game Cookbook

A MENU COOKBOOK

Also by Rebecca Gray

American Artisanal:
Finding the Country's Best Real Food, from Cheese to Chocolate

Chefs Go Wild:
The Best Fish and Game Recipes on the Planet

Eat Like a Wild Man:
110 Years of Great Game and Fish Recipes

Gray's Fish Cookbook:
A Menu Cookbook

Gray's Wild Game Cookbook:
A Menu Cookbook

Venison

When Fishermen Cook Fish

As contributing editor:

Joy of Cooking:
75th Anniversary Edition

The New Gray's Wild Game Cookbook

A MENU COOKBOOK

Rebecca Gray

GrayBooks
Lyme, New Hampshire

Text Copyright © 2009 Rebecca Gray
Illustrations Copyright © 2009 DeCourcy Taylor Jr.
All rights reserved.

ISBN-10: 0-9841471-4-4
ISBN-13: 978-0-9841471-4-4
Library of Congress Catalog Number: 2009907934

Published by
GrayBooks LLC
1 Main Street
Lyme, New Hampshire 03768
www.GrayBooksPublishers.com

First Edition
Softcover

Printed in The Unites States of America
on acid-free paper.

As it was for the first and will be till the last...
For Edward

Contents

Acknowledgments — xiv
Preface — 17

Venison 23

Venison Black Bean Chili — 28
    Baby Spinach and Arugula Salad with Avocado and Egg
    Fennel Seed Bread
    Ginger Angel Crisps

Venison Burgers with Chateaubriand Butter — 33
    Fried Bread
    Vegetable Salad
    Fresh Fruit

Saddle of Venison — 36
    Potatoes and Porcini
    Braised Fennel
    Clafoutis

Venison Strip Steaks — 39
    Fried Potato Skins
    Grilled Red Pepper Salad
    Strawberry Ice Cream

Venison Stew — 42
    Homemade Pasta
    Crusted Blueberry and Cream Cake

Venison Stew with Artichoke Hearts and Sun-dried Tomatoes — 46
    Basil Bread
    Green Salad
    Custard Oranges

Venison with Port — 50
    Roast Potatoes
    Sautéed Watercress
    Meyer Lemon Sherbet

Venison Scallops   52
    Persillade Potatoes
    Green Beans
    Tarte Tatin

Venison Chops with Pignolis and Red Peppers   54
    Pepperoni Bread
    Green Salad
    Stuffed Oranges

Venison Chops with Mustard Butter   57
    Roast Potatoes with Rosemary
    Green Beans and Beet Salad
    Coffee Granita

Venison Steak with Wild Mushrooms   60
    Blue Cheese Polenta
    Spinach and Bibb Lettuce Salad
    Strawberry Ice

Venison Steaks Marinated   62
    Grilled Red Pepper Salad
    Mashed Potatoes with Fresh Basil
    Vanilla Ice Cream with Homemade Butterscotch Sauce

Grilled Venison Steak with Rosemary Butter   67
    Bibb Lettuce and Tomato Salad
    White Bean Purée
    Coffee Ice Cream and Hazelnut Liqueur

Venison Chops with Blue Cheese and Caraway Seeds   69
    Sweet Potato Gratin
    Braised Fennel
    Fresh Figs

Venison Steak with Red Wine   71
    Bittergreens and Cheese Salad
    Garlic Toasts
    Rhubarb Tart

Venison Calzone   74
    Sliced Tomatoes with Basil
    Fried Sage Leaves
    Poached Pears

Venison Chops with Basil Cream   77
    Homemade Pasta with Parsley
    Salad with Hazelnut Dressing
    Brandied Apricots and Crème Anglaise

Upland Birds   81

Grilled Breast of Sandhill Crane   86
    Green Beans and Beet Salad
    Mascarpone Risotto
    Chocolate Gelato

Quail for the Campfire   88
    Grilled Red Onion
    Charcoal Grilled Bread
    Almond Cake

Green Grape Quail   90
    Wild Rice with Walnuts
    Sliced Tomatoes with Fresh Basil
    Crème Brulée

Grouse Pancetta   93
    Julienned Celery and Zucchini
    Fried Polenta
    Poached Prunes and Apricots with Cognac and Cream

Spitted Woodcock   96
    Green Beans with Wild Mushrooms
    Baked Goat Cheese
    Meyer Lemon Sherbet

Dove Salad   100
    Cornsticks
    Tangerine Sorbet

Fried Dove   102
    Zucchini with Tomato
    Gorgonzola Polenta
    Toll House Cookies

Preserved Woodcock with Olives   104
    Basil Pasta
    Sun-dried Tomato Bread
    Cantaloupe Ice

Juniper Encrusted Woodcock in Rosemary Cream Sauce 108
 Leg of Lamb
 White Bean Purée
 Green Salad
 Stuffed Oranges

Quail Soup 110
 Pasta with Chestnuts and Pignolis
 Olive Oil and Salt Bread
 Custard Oranges

Pheasant Sandwich 114
 Ruffed Grouse Sandwich with Hazelnut Butter
 Cold Wild Rice Salad
 Assorted Cheeses (Brie, Goat, Saga)
 Olives
 Fresh Fruit
 Cookies and Cheese

Roast Wild Turkey 117
 Fontina Polenta
 Fava Beans, Peas and Pancetta
 Green Salad
 Rhubarb Tart

Pheasant in Wine 120
 Fiddleheads
 Baked Grits
 Strawberry Tart

Grilled Quail 124
 Grilled Mushrooms
 Purée of Peas
 Pear Cake

Quick Grilled Quail 127
 Sautéed Watercress
 Cauliflower and Mayonnaise
 Chocolate Cake

Pheasant Salad 130
 Soup in a Pumpkin
 Basil Bread
 Figs in Rum

Pheasant and Cabbage   134
    Cooked Apples
    Cheese

Woodcock Armagnac on Garlic Toasts   136
    Fennel and Peas
    Roast Potatoes
    Tarte Tatin

Chukar Stuffed with Hazelnuts   139
    Grated Zucchini
    Sautéed Cherry Tomatoes
    Cheese, Thyme Toasts
    Fresh Fruit

Water Fowl 143

Duck with Ginger and Scallions   146
    Sautéed Watercress
    Cheese, Thyme Toast
    Chocolate Cake

Ducks with Rosemary and Sage   149
    Fontina Polenta
    Zucchini Fans with Tomatoes
    Coffee Ice Cream with Frangelico

Grilled Sea Ducks   152
    Grilled Vegetables
    Garlic Cheese Bread
    Poached Pears

Grilled Breast of Mallard   154
    Gorgonzola Polenta
    Cucumber and Radishes
    Fresh Fruit

Stuffed Duck Breasts   156
    Green Beans and Wild Mushrooms
    Bibb and Radish Salad
    Grapefruit Sabayon

Duck Salad   158
    Basil Pasta
    Cantaloupe Ice

Grilled Marinated Ducks 162
 Grilled Red Onion
 Grilled Mushrooms
 Basil Bread
 Crème Brulée

Roasted Duck 166
 Potatoes Steamed with Sage
 Bittergreens and Cheese Salad
 Tangerine Sorbet

Minted Roast Duck with Potatoes, Carrots and Turnips 169
 Green Salad
 Alice Waters' Olive Oil and Sauternes Cake

Duck Roasted with Red Pepper Butter 171
 Persillade Potatoes
 Sautéed Green Beans and Cherry Tomatoes
 Almond Cake

Sea Duck Fricassee 173
 Fennel, Mint, Cucumber, Radish Salad
 Fried Polenta
 Fresh Fruit

Sea Duck with Pancetta and Prosciutto 176
 Roast Potatoes with Rosemary
 Fresh Green Peas
 Kiwi Ice

Grilled Breast of Duck with Wild Mushrooms 178
  and Honey Mustard Sauce
 Soup in a Pumpkin
 Olive Oil and Salt Bread
 Figs in Rum

Marinated Duck Breasts 182
 Plain Roast Potatoes
 Julienned Celery and Zucchini
 Strawberry Tart

Grilled Lemon Duck 185
 Grated Zucchini
 Sautéed Cherry Tomatoes
 Grilled Bread
 Pear Cake

Smoked Goose Salad   188
    Butternut Squash Soup
    Sun-dried Tomato Bread
    Chocolate Cake

Smoked Goose In Cold Pasta Salad   193
    Pepperoni Bread
    Almond Cake

Christmas Goose Anytime   196
    Pignolis and Raisin Cognac Stuffing
    Sautéed Mustard Greens
    Cooked Apples
    Cornsticks
    Good Floating Island

Mixed Bag   201

Roast Leg of Mountain Goat   204
    Blue Cheese Polenta
    Mixed Green Salad
    Alice Waters' Olive Oil and Sauternes Cake

Braised Bear   207
    Baby Artichokes
    Fava Beans, Peas, and Pancetta
    Fresh Fruit

Boar Chops with Pernod and Mustard Butter   210
    Gaufrette Potatoes
    Fiddleheads
    Raspberry Tart

Roast Sheep   213
    Sautéed Watercress
    Pasta with Chestnuts and Pignolis
    Poached Prunes and Apricots with Cognac and Cream

Braised Rabbit   216
    Sautéed Cucumbers
    Red Peppers with Basil
    Clafoutis

Rabbit Salad   219
    Black Olive Bread
    Baked Apples with Crème Anglaise
Boar with Ginger and Orange Sauce   222
    Fried Bread
    Fried Sage Leaves
    Good Floating Island
Game Bird Sausage with Rhubarb-Port Syrup   225
    Pasta with Fresh Chanterelles
    Sautéed Watercress
    Pistachio Gelato

Game Care 229

There's More to a Menu Than the Game 237

Menus for After a Day of Hunting	237
Menus For the Great Outdoors	239
Menus That Are Ooh La La	240
Menus for People Who Have Never Eaten Game and Don't Eat Things That Walk Sideways or Grow In the Dark	242
Just For the Two of You	244
And to Feed an Army or Hunting Party ...	245

A Few Suggestions 247

Index 257

Acknowledgments

Of course at the core of *The New Gray's Wild Game Cookbook* are the recipes and menus that Cintra Reeve and I created more than twenty-five years ago for the very first *Gray's Sporting Journal* game cookbook. Consequently this new book—indeed much of my culinary training—is in large measure a product of Cintra's influence, her superior professional chef skills, guidance, and creativity in the kitchen. So I thank Cintra first and foremost here for her long-ago help, but also for giving me a wonderful foundation for what has become a lifelong passion for me, that of cooking and writing about food, especially all things wild.

Where Cintra was at the start of my foodie writings so were there others at the beginning. Two people in particular helped me back then and now again have allowed their contributions to reappear here in the new game cookbook. My thanks to Frank Foster who for years did the food photography for our magazine, *Gray's Sporting Journal*, and allowed us to use his dust jacket cover photo again for this book. Also, thank you DeCourcy "Larry" Taylor for letting us include your lovely pencil drawings again. But perhaps more importantly, Larry, you have my gratitude for imparting your beautiful sense of design and typography into everything "Gray's"—it still shines through today in this book.

As with hunting and fishing, cooking and writing about food is a continuous learning process, evolving over a lifetime. So it is I wish to acknowledge the editors of my other wild game cookbooks, written over several decades, who have so skillfully contributed to my process: Tom Petrie, Terry McDonell, Sid Evans, Jay Cassell, and also Beth Wareham and Susan and Ethan Becker who invited me to participate in the 75th anniversary edition of the *Joy of Cooking*. All of these fine folks not only provided encouragement and let stand in writing my rather strong opinions on wild food, but also reminded me to put myself in the boots and kitchen of my audience—

the great readers, hunters, eaters, and cooks like you. I believe their influence has helped me make this a better book.

Yet none of this would have happened without Ed. From the first wild game cookbook to the latest one—and with much that came before, between, and after—his enthusiasm, brilliance, and vision is what inspires and makes so much a reality for me. My best editor, best dinner guest, best mentor, best friend, best partner in all parts of an extraordinary and wonderful life together—for Ed there simply aren't adequate words.

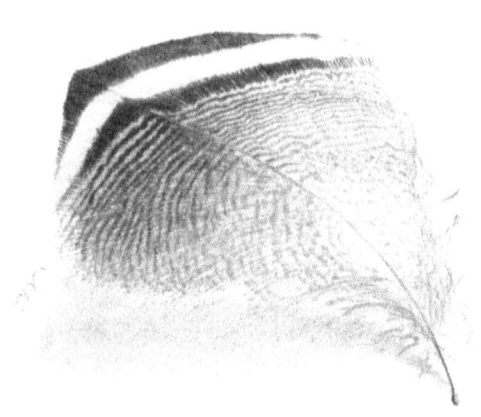

Preface

Revising this, my out-of-print game cookbook—written some twenty-five years ago and my very first book—has been sort of traumatic. In my mind I kept likening it to what I'd heard happens when a person is drowning: A whole lot of your life—the good and bad experiences—flash before your eyes making you at once grimace at your own innocence and ignorance and euphoric at the beauty of a good life. Fortunately, in the case of cookbook revisions the good that flashed before me was in the context of preparing fish and game and any of the naïve or embarrassing stuff I was able with wild abandon to simply cut from the pages and—just like that—from my life, too!

Actually, the edits and refreshes had to be done to make this cookbook accurate. I don't mean accurate so much in terms of numbers of tablespoons or cooking times, although that was good to revisit, too, or because the world has moved on in its culinary sophistication—now you can actually buy sun-dried tomatoes everywhere! But I want this cookbook to be a reflection of me, here and now, not just me when I was thirty-something and wrote the first edition, but me as a sixty year old. My bias, passion, and opinion—and yes, my experiential knowledge—is much more definitive now that I'm sixty. And yes and hurrah, this is especially so in the context of cooking and eating wild.

Naturally much of what I wrote in the preface of that first *Gray's Wild Game Cookbook* remains true and the basis for the way I think about cooking game. Hunting and wild game preparation were not a tradition in my family. But my father and grandfather and great-grandfather had spent their business lives in Chicago's meat-processing industry. I'd seen the seven blue stomachs of a steer fall on the floor of a Kansas City slaughter house, smelled a chicken rendering plant in Iowa, and knew exactly what really went into those hotdog casings. Even still I was not prepared for a feathered, slightly bloody carcass in my kitchen. I prided myself on developing a sophisticated palate at an early age and had willingly tasted turtle steak, whale meat and fish tongues, but I was uneasy when I took my first bite of woodcock. And if apprehension over the bird's unconventional appearance and unusual flavor were not enough to put me off, then the fact that it was impossible to cook sure did. What cookbooks I could find on game didn't seem to speak to me: Does sour cream or canned cream of mushroom soup have to be in every recipe? Am I told to use a meat grinder because the author's never heard of a food processor? Has the author *tasted* a goose smoked for eight hours? What vegetables go with bear?

Of course, in the now many years since that first feathered carcass, experience has not only lessened my apprehensions, but made it possible for me to go on from this initial cookbook to writing and editing many more after that. Learning to hunt, being involved in the writing and production of the cooking feature for *Gray's Sporting Journal*, experimenting with all kinds of recipes plus exchanging ideas about cooking game with outdoor writers, artists, hunt club cooks, outfitters, gun manufacturers, caterers, and professional chefs has basically eliminated the trepidation. The anxiety has been replaced with a good bit of knowledge and a love for folks sitting around my table, enjoying the company, the food and discussing days in the kitchen and in the field—and the joy of bringing it to the table.

My education definitely evolved, but always came back to the same tenet: great ingredients are the basis for all good meals and game is intrinsically a great ingredient. In the early years of publishing *Gray's Sporting Journal*, our very well-known writer friend and *Gray's* contributor, Charley Waterman, came to visit. So knowledgeable, so lucid, so funny, Charley was in many ways the ideal for the role of mentor. As I drove Charley from the airport through the wilds of the Boston city streets, I picked his brain on everything from how a husband goes about teaching a wife to enjoy hunting to my favorite topic, cooking game. What was Charley's preferred quail recipe, how long did he and Debie cook a duck, how long did they hang their venison? My brain raced with questions, firing one after another at Charley, only to get the simple reply: "We don't do much of anything to our game, just cook it."

Then it happened again. We'd befriended the famous wildlife watercolorist Chet Reneson and his wife, Penny. Chet's artwork often appeared on the cover of our magazine and Penny, to my mind the perfect wife to a hunter and fisherman, became a role model for me. She would know there was no way to anticipate the end to a hunter's day (they were always late); or when to assert her own desire—or not—to hunt. She understood all those moments of quandary—and she *really* knew how to cook. I admired her for all her common sense and abilities. One evening as we drove to a Ducks Unlimited dinner, I had the opportunity to ask her about my new topic of choice, cooking game. "We don't do much of anything to our game," she said, "just cook it."

Of course, when pressed, both Charley and Penny had some quite definite ideas about game cooking, but nonetheless there was a common message to be had from both of them: When cooking good-quality game the best results are achieved by doing little else but applying heat. And, however incongruous a statement that might seem in a cookbook, it is accurate. Let the good stuff shine and don't muck it up with a lot of extraneous stuff. It is also why I've tried to keep the recipes and menus here simple. (Now a mediocre piece of game can require more attention—a more involved recipe, so keep reading the book.) My focus is on the ingredients, not on the complexity of the recipes. It is in the end always about good ingredients.

In addition to the expansion of my own experience and influences from the hunting world, something else happened which affected the revision of this book. In the late 1970s and into the early 1980s—when I wrote the first edition—it was a rare restaurant that served any type of game. A specialty store might carry an occasional farm-raised quail, pheasant or rabbit, but again it was unusual. Of course, the laws prevented any hunted species from being sold, so the rarity of game was partially due to lack of supply, but clearly also lack of demand. Yet it all began to change in the 1990s. Quite suddenly game became very popular. I've speculated as to why this happened and have several theories: the health benefits of fatless game; the movement toward organic, chemically untainted meats; increased interest and support of local foods; that eating game can be kind of titillating and thrilling. Or was game now being served by chefs in search of a new star on the culinary stage with which to impress their worldly and increasingly knowledgeable clientele? Or had the explosion of game farms caused more game to be served in restaurants—which came first, the pheasant or the egg farm? Likely it was all of the above. As a hunter and game cook I was at first slightly annoyed, even arrogant, about *faux* wild game. The game farms and their homogenized pen-raised birds couldn't stand up to the real thing. Only birds feeding on worms, twigs, wild berries and the like, shot and then field-dressed by my own hand—or a friend's—counted as wild in my books. Then in 1998 I wrote a book about venison and used farm-raised cuts for the photos. The venison was supplied by D'Artagnan—the well-known purveyor of game, primarily to restaurants. The photographer, a woman friend named Christopher Hirsheimer, was also an editor of the food magazine, *SAVEUR*, and a very accomplished cook. Together we cooked and styled the photos and then ate the venison; it was delicious. And the "aha" here was that it was available on demand, not just the year that Ed shot a deer! There was now endless opportunity to experiment with game.

And the availability of farmed game also expanded the pool of chefs who were also experimenting and using game for new creations, as I learned when I started writing a column for *Shooting Sportsman* magazine. For the column, I wrote about professional chefs—usually hunters themselves—who featured game on their menus. I discovered that for most of these chefs wild was a broad and evocative descriptor, not a technical term. There is a difference, and all who cook game know it—the truly wild are lean and fatless—and I will always have my bias on the flavor difference. But what farm-raised game fosters is a perpetuation of the culinary sensibilities that are inherent in cooking truly wild game. Cooking game—wild or not—is interesting, often challenging, exciting, founded in culinary history and can provide an intense and thought-provoking experience in eating which we can't get from grocery store beef or chicken.

So now what? What has twenty-five plus years now brought to *The New Gray's Wild Game Cookbook*? Some changes in techniques, some updates in ingredients, and additional recipes and menus have been incorporated into what was originally here. But more importantly I believe there's a new clarity for me now in the purpose of cooking game, which I pass along here. I think I best stated it in a memo I wrote a couple of years ago to Beth Wareham. Beth was the editor of the 75th anniversary edition of the *Joy of Cooking* and hired me to be the expert editor on the game and other wild edible sections of the *Joy*. This is what I wrote initially to her:

> First, so you know how I approached this section of the *Joy of Cooking*, here is my general attitude about wild edibles: Wild game should not be cooked so the diners

exclaim, "It tastes just like chicken!" Wild fowl are not chickens. To treat as such you run the risk of making it taste like chicken, or worse. The ADVANTAGE of wild game is that it has unusual, more robust flavor, different textures, and is often unpredictable, which makes it exciting to both eat and cook. We should celebrate and enhance this in how we treat a gamebird. It is important to remain flexible, adventuresome and thoughtful when preparing wild foods. Since it is wild, you have no information on or assurance that there was anything but a rough, stressful existence in the creature's past. The rules may already have been broken in proper game care. However, let's not make it sound scary, icky or too far from the familiar. It is unethical to kill something and not intend to eat it. (If it is old and therefore less succulent, it still should be eaten. But there can be good reasons, too, to discard.) Cooking game teaches us to be better cooks, involves us more intimately and thoughtfully in what we are about to cook and eat. In the last decade game has become increasingly more popular and more readily available in restaurants and grocery stores. Just like the *Joy*, wild game cooking has a long and significant role in America's culinary history. Unlike anything else, game is ultimately the most American ingredient, the only possible food capable of establishing itself as a defining element in a true American cuisine. It is important to know about.

So this is what game cooking is all about for me. That attitude goes with *The New Gray's Wild Game Cookbook*. I hope the book inspires, makes you laugh, teaches you something, entertains, and most importantly, makes you want to cook wild.

Venison

I haven't always known about cooking venison. A culinary confrontation with a piece of venison in the late 1960s got me going: a white-tailed deer steak that mysteriously appeared at the Tufts University fraternity house in Boston where a boyfriend lived and where I spent a lot of time. This was back before college-age men thought it was cool to be a good cook and so the task of preparing food unquestioningly fell to the woman on hand—in this case, me. I recall there were deer hairs on the steak, a clear sign that the last person who'd handled the meat knew even less than I did about game prep. But while I carefully picked each hair off, I noticed something else: Despite whatever it had been through, it was absolutely beautiful, rich, lean meat. I don't remember—likely because it was pretty unmemorable—how I actually cooked it or even how the venison tasted. Fraternity evenings have a way of provoking forgetfulness, but still this void in my culinary knowledge, and probably some vague sense that venison could be spectacular eating, piqued my curiosity: How *do* you prepare venison?

The fraternity venison incident also foreshadowed what was to come—initially a necessary learning process, but eventually a life-long passion. In 1975 I married a hunter and fisherman, and the same year of our marriage Ed and I started our publication, *Gray's Sporting Journal*. Suddenly I was faced not only with game in my kitchen but with editing a cooking feature for our hunting and fishing magazine. And quickly I was again faced with the preparation conundrums of venison. Only now it wasn't just cooking problems; I had to help tackle the job of cleaning birds or butchering a whole deer carcass. I was into it now—if only for the imperative moral and ethical rationale that you eat what you kill—and committed to learning everything about game, every subtlety of preparing and cooking it.

The word venison is derived from the Latin verb *venari*, to hunt. And in Robin Hood-type olden days, venison actually referred to all game—meat of an animal killed in the chase. Now we're more explicit, defining the deer species as venison. And although it seems less obvious, we include moose, elk, and caribou in the venison group. These are three of the five species of *Cervidae* (antlered herbivores of the *Artiodactyla* order) which are indigenous to North America. The other two are mule and white-tailed deer, whitetails being the dominant and oldest of the North America deer species.

Deer were indispensable to the early Native Americans. Influencing the spiritual, cultural and economic elements of tribal life, venison was also a substantial portion of their diet. At an archeological site in West Virginia indications are that about ninety percent of the meat being eaten there was venison—and it wasn't only everyday fare. At the 1623 wedding of Plymouth Colony Governor William Bradford, the Wampanoag Indians brought gifts of deer. "We had about twelve pasty venison [meat pies], besides others," wrote one of the guests, Emmanuel Altham, "[and] pieces of roast venison and other such good cheer in such quantity that I could wish you some of our share."

There was such heavy deer harvesting in colonial times that by 1800 the herds had been reduced by thirty-five to fifty percent from pre-Columbian estimates. Between the years of 1776 and 1850 the population of Americans increased from 1.5 million to 23 million, all of them consuming vast quantities of wild game. Plus, venison was inexpensive, which added more pressure on the resource. In 1868 venison was actually cheaper to buy than beef or pork and by the 1890s the harvesting of deer—often by market hunters—was unparalleled by any other time in our history.

By the early 1900s, the entire deer population in the U.S. numbered only 500,000. And deer were not the only game being slaughtered: ducks, geese, turkey, grouse, quail and buffalo all faced near-extinction from over-harvesting. In response a federal regulation, the Lacey Act was passed which prohibited interstate commerce of game taken in violation of state law. The Act basically ended the practice of market hunting, thus saving much of our wildlife. So for most of the 20th Century virtually the only way to eat American venison was if you, or a sharing friend, could successfully hunt deer.

The history of venison in Europe was quite different: Venison was the stuff of kings—no democratic freedoms for the masses when it came to deer hunting or consumption. Hunting was strictly controlled by the ruling class, who limited the number of deer harvested and initiated habitat management to secure herd size. Then in the process of colonizing other parts of the world, the Europeans not only found new species of deer, but enjoyed the freedom to hunt them.

In the mid-1800s the British transplanted red, fallow and sika deer to New Zealand, primarily for recreational hunting, and the deer found ideal habitat. They prospered to the point that their exploding population all but denuded the hills of vegetation, causing extensive erosion, habitat loss, and near extinction of some ground-feeding birds. Within a little over a hundred years the deer grew so pervasive they were not only hunted extensively but poisoned as pests. Then some enterprising hunters decided that instead of letting the plentiful deer carcasses just rot, they would sell them to restaurants. This caught the attention of New Zealand farmers and in the first true domestication of a wild species in over 10,000 years, farmers captured and then propagated deer. By 1987 there were 3,500 deer farms in New Zealand and over 860,000 pounds of the Kiwi venison being served in U.S. restaurants.

There'd been a growing desire and interest here in new cuisines and all things culinary, which got its start when World War II troops returned from Europe. First it had to be French, then Italian, then any ethnic, exotic or gourmet food. It was fueled in the 1960s by the television. show of Cordon Bleu-trained Julia Child, and later in the 1980s redefined by Alice Waters' emphasis on artisanal foods of the *terroir*. Certainly this progression helped drive the demand in the U.S for Euro-exotic venison. From 1990 to 1994 our venison consumption doubled. Sure, venison's popularity was due in large part to our blossoming appreciation of gourmet foods, but also to the burgeoning emphasis on healthy, more natural foods. Venison is high in protein, contains iron, zinc and many of the B vitamins; and it's raised naturally—devoid of growth hormones, antibiotics and dyes. Plus venison is very lean, with one-eighth the fat content of beef and less cholesterol than a skinless chicken breast.

With an increasing demand for venison here in the U.S., the opportunity door was open for a domestic supply to find its way into the marketplace. During the 20th Century there had been an incredible rebound of wild American deer: from a total population of half a million in 1900 to 25 million in 1997. By 2006 the white-tailed deer alone was estimated to be close to 20 million animals. Despite this, the Lacey Act has remained intact, preventing any commercial use of wild game. But the Lacey Act has no jurisdiction over farm-raised animals.

Are there differences between wild and farm-raised deer? Of course. Farm-raised deer are fenced in and more sedentary than their wild counterparts. Plus the constancy of their diet and the slaughterhouse approach to processing the meat all make for a different flavor—farmed venison is a bit flatter, less, well…flavorful. In general, we've domesticated the taste right out of most of our meat, and farmed venison seems headed in that direction.

I admit bias here. Since those early deer days, I'd seized the challenge, grabbed the gauntlet and spent decades learning how to prepare game. And included in my new venison knowledge were techniques and opinions about processing—proper bleeding, cooling, aging, butchering. It was always wild deer and I was picky about it, downright snooty, shuddering at the very memory of my two firsts—the fraternity hair-flecked steak and the cartop deer (see "Game Care," p. 229). Now I knew what made great venison— its wildness made the complexities, subtle nuances of flavor that were unparalleled. And the way we handled it, I'm proud to say, encouraged that nuanced and fabulous taste.

In this chapter we have not been quite as liberal with the term venison as in the Robin Hood days, but do use the word venison in its broader sense to mean all that are in the deer family: caribou, moose, elk, antelope, whitetail and mule deer. This is a cook's taxonomy, not a biologist's, so all of the venison recipes in this chapter are applicable to these animals. Some slight adjustments in quantities of accompanying ingredients and cooking times should be made to accommodate for a larger size (moose, elk) cut of venison.

Venison Black Bean Chili
Baby Spinach and Arugula Salad with Avocado and Egg
Fennel Seed Bread
Ginger Angel Crisps

Serves eight

VENISON BLACK BEAN CHILI

- 2 cups black beans, dried or 3 16-oz. cans
- ¼ cup oil, approximately
- 1 stalk celery, chopped small
- 2 medium onions, chopped small
- 8 cloves garlic, chopped very fine
- 4 lbs. boneless venison cut in ½-inch cubes
- 1 tsp. salt
- 3 tbsp. dried oregano
- 1 tsp. cayenne pepper
- ½ tsp. ground coriander
- ⅓ cup medium-hot chili powder
- 2 tbsp. ground cumin
- 3½ cups hot chicken stock (use Knorr chicken cubes)
- 1 28-oz. can Italian plum tomatoes
- Approximately 8 cups cooked, short grain, brown rice (or you can use wild rice if you are feeling lavish)
- 3-4 tbsp. chopped parsley for garnish
- 1 cup sour cream mixed with grated rind of 1 lemon to be passed as garnish (optional)

Rinse the dried beans, remove any stones and cover with water in a large pot and bring to a boil. Remove from the heat , cover and let stand several hours. Then drain , cover with water again and cook for 1-2 hours until they are tender but still have some bite. (Some beans are tougher than others, especially ones from health food stores which should definitely be soaked overnight.) If using canned beans, just rinse well and drain.

Heat half of the oil in a large cooking casserole and cook the celery and the onions over medium heat till soft, about 15 minutes. Add the garlic and cook another few minutes, stirring, then remove all from the pan to a small bowl.

Heat the rest of the oil in the same pan, add the meat and cook stirring occasionally until the meat is grey—you do not sear the meat so use medium heat, it should take no longer than 10-15 minutes.

Then return the onion mixture to the pan and add salt, oregano, cayenne, coriander, chili powder, and cumin. Stir to mix and cook another 5 minutes.

Now add the stock and canned tomatoes (break them with a fork) with their juices; bring to a boil. Stir well and simmer uncovered for 2 hours or until the meat is folk-tender.

Stir in the beans and taste for seasoning. You probably will want more salt and oregano. Heat until nice and hot and serve with rice, parsley and/or lemon sour cream.

If you want to thicken the juices, place a tablespoon or so of cornstarch in a glass and mix with a few tablespoons of water. Then add a few teaspoons of the hot chili liquid; one by one. Mix well, pour it all back into the pot and slowly bring to a boil stirring all the time—-then remove from the heat. It should thicken right up. Just remember if you should reheat the chili, do so slowly, so as not to break the starch.

BABY SPINACH AND ARUGULA SALAD WITH AVOCADO AND EGG

For the vinaigrette:
- 1 tbsp. lemon juice
- 1 tbsp. balsamic vinegar
- ¼ tsp. salt
- Several grinds of the pepper grinder
- 1 tsp. prepared honey mustard
- ¼ cup good green olive oil

For the salad
- 1 hard-cooked egg
- 1 bag baby spinach leaves
- 1 bag baby arugula
- 1 ripe avocado

Combine all six ingredients for the vinaigrette in a small jar with a lid that fits securely. Make sure the lid is on tight and shake vigorously several times before using it to dress the salad.

Set the egg in water and cook on high for 17 minutes. Remove from the heat and put the egg under cold running water. While the egg is cooking, wash and spin dry both the spinach and arugula and place in a salad bowl. Peel and slice both the egg and the avocado and add it to the spinach/arugula. Dress with the vinaigrette and toss. Add a few grinds of the pepper grinder.

FENNEL SEED BREAD

- 2 cups lukewarm to warm water
- 1 tbsp. dry yeast
- 1 tbsp. sugar
- 1 tbsp. salt
- 2 tbsp. dried fennel seed, plus enough to sprinkle atop each loaf
- 5 cups or so of all-purpose flour (I recommend King Arthur Flour)
- Butter and oil for greasing pans

In the bowl of a standing mix master, fitted with a bread hook, add the warm water and sprinkle in the yeast, sugar, salt, and 2 tbsp. fennel seed. Let sit for a few minutes until the yeast looks dissolved and foamy. Now pour in 5 cups of flour and mix at the lowest setting, usually marked "stir," until the flour is blended and then increase the speed to the next level, #2. Continue blending at this speed until the dough is well mixed, pulling away from the sides of the bowl, and forming a ball. Turn onto a floured surface and knead the dough for about 8 minutes. It should be slightly tacky to the touch but smooth and very malleable. Place in a bowl that has been oiled, turn the dough over in the oil so the top is oiled, too, and cover the bowl with a cloth. Let rise until it is double in size, about 2 to 3 hours. Punch it down and let it rest while you prepare the pan(s) for it to rise in again.

This recipe makes enough for a baguette and a loaf. I always make a baguette for the week's spaghetti night so I pull a handful of dough off and roll it into a big snake and lay it in one side of a baguette pan that has been buttered. The remaining dough I either place into a buttered loaf pan, pushing it into the rectangle shape, or form a ball with the dough, flouring it heavily, and put into a banneton, also heavily floured. Both the baguette and the loaf/round I cover with a cloth and let rise again for another hour or so.

The breads in the metal baking pans can first be sprinkled with fennel seeds and then go directly into a preheated oven at 420° for 35 to 40 minutes until golden brown. The banneton is trickier. I use a piece of parchment paper, floured, atop the back of a cookie sheet and carefully invert the banneton and let the dough fall out. Often it loses its rise and I let it sit covered for another hour to rise again. Once the round is ready to bake I sprinkle it with fennel seeds and slide it onto a pizza stone that is in a preheated oven at 420° and bake it for 40 minutes or until golden. Once baked, I turn the baguette and loaf out of their pans—or slide the round on the parchment onto the cookie sheet—and onto a rack to cool. Let cool for 30 minutes or so before cutting.

If I don't plan to use the baguette that day I wrap it in foil and put it in the freezer to use another day. (It just needs to be taken from the freezer and put in a preheated oven at 350° for 30 minutes or so.)

GINGER ANGEL CRISPS

- 1½ cups flour
- ½ tsp. baking soda
- ¼ cup (½ stick) unsalted butter
- ¼ cup sugar
- ½ cup molasses
- ½ tsp. powdered ginger
- Powdered sugar for dusting (about a ½ cup)

In a bowl combine the flour and baking soda and whisk it a few times to mix and set aside. In a medium-size pan bring to a rolling boil the butter, sugar, molasses, and ginger and let it boil a minute or two. Remove from the heat and stir in the flour mixture a little at a time until it is completely incorporated. Let the dough cool just a bit—it should still be very warm to the touch—and take a large spoonful and form into a ball. Set on a lightly floured surface and cover with plastic wrap. Roll out the dough so it is VERY thin. Remove the wrap and using a little angel—or other small form—cookie cutter, cut out the cookies. Place the angels on a cookie sheet lined with parchment paper and cook in a preheated oven at 350º for 4 to 8 minute or until the edges are browning slightly. Remove from the oven and slide the parchment with the cookies onto a cooling rack. Let sit for 5 minutes and then slide Angel Crisps from the paper onto a plate. In a small plastic bag pour a small amount of powdered sugar and add, in batches of 3, the little angel cookies and shake to cover.

Repeat with remaining dough. (After a while you may have to re-heat the dough, it needs to be very warm in order to roll it thin.) This makes a good number of cookies—certainly enough for eight people—but the precise number depends on the size of your angels.

Venison Burgers with Chateaubriand Butter
Fried Bread
Vegetable Salad
Fresh Fruit

Serves four

Venison burger is not only delightful to eat, but often your best alternative for the cuts damaged in the field or naturally tougher. If the outfitter has not butchered the deer for you and you fancy doing it yourself, you may find it difficult getting the meat made into burger. If you are a city-dweller and hunting refers to what shoppers do at Bloomie's or Macy's rather than something that goes on in the woods, chances are you will not find a butcher who will grind the meat for you. Even the la-di-da butchers who have gouged you for years and theoretically owe you a favor are bound by the state sanitary codes and don't like to risk any infringement of the law.

Rural butchers are likelier to be able to handle your request to grind the meat and add the pork fat necessary to create burger. If you are going to try to grind it yourself, I make two suggestions. Try to use meat that is very cold—near freezing—and free of any fat or sinew. A food processor works well, as does the meat grinder attachment to a Kitchen Aid mixer. But I once spent a tearful evening, when I was pregnant with our third child and Ed was off hunting, trying to jam big chunks of deer leg meat through a hand-crank meat grinder. It simply did not work. In general grinding meat at home is tedious and better to do in small batches or left to the butcher or outfitter to do. (For more on grinding, see page 253)

VENISON BURGERS WITH CHATEAUBRIAND BUTTER

- 1 cup white wine
- 3 shallots chopped very, very fine
- 1 handful of fresh parsley, chopped
- 1 tsp. chervil
- 1 tsp. tarragon
- 1 cup stock
- 1 cup (2 sticks) unsalted butter
- Salt and pepper
- 2 lbs. venison burger (chopped or ground)

In a small saucepan combine the wine, shallot, parsley, chervil, and tarragon and bring it to a boil. Reduce heat and simmer very, very slowly until the liquid has been reduced by half. Add the stock and continue to reduce until ½ cup liquid is left. Whip the butter till soft and add the cooled wine and stock mixture. Season with salt and pepper and wrap in plastic wrap. Shape into a log and freeze one hour or overnight. Form the burger into patties and cook over a grill. Slice several pats of the butter for each burger and serve on top.

FRIED BREAD

- 1 loaf French bread
- 1 garlic clove
- ½ cup (1 stick) unsalted butter
- Salt to taste

Slice the French bread into 12 ½-inch pieces and dry them on a cookie sheet in a 300° oven. Do not let them cook. If you wish, rub one side of the dried bread with a garlic clove sliced in half. In a heavy-bottomed saucepan, melt the stick of butter, heating it till it sizzles. Put in the bread and brown both sides. Sprinkle with salt if you like.

VEGETABLE SALAD

    1 14-oz. can artichoke hearts
    ½ lb. fava beans
    ½ lb. peas
    ½ lb. new potatoes

Drain, rinse and quarter the artichoke hearts. Shell, peel and blanch the fava beans. Plunge into cold water. Shell and blanch the peas. Plunge into cold water. When both fava beans and peas are cool combine with the artichoke. Cook the little potatoes in enough salted boiling water to just cover them for 20 minutes or until tender. Let cool and then quarter them. Add the potatoes to the other vegetables and then toss with a nice herbed vinaigrette.

Saddle of Venison
Potatoes and Porcini
Braised Fennel
Clafoutis

Serves four

It took me years to find out what was meant by a "saddle of venison." I had heard of a rack or a haunch but never a saddle. A saddle of venison is the equivalent of a standing rib roast in beef. It is the middle section of chops left intact to make the premier of roasts. At the point of butchering the saddle can cause the very worst consternation. Whether 'tis nobler to wade through a series of delicious meals of venison chops or to go for the glut of an incredible roast—if you go for the glut we suggest the following recipe.

SADDLE OF VENISON

- ¼ cup olive oil
- 1 tbsp. lemon juice
- 5-6 lbs. saddle of venison
- Enough pork lard to cover the saddle
- 1 tbsp. crushed juniper berries
- 1 tsp. salt
- 1 onion, sliced
- 5 tbsp. unsalted butter
- ¼ cup red wine vinegar
- 1 lemon
- Sprinkle of flour
- Salt and pepper

Combine the oil and lemon juice and rub over the meat. Let it sit for a couple of hours. Lard with 2-inch strips in even rows with pork fat. Mix the juniper berries and salt together and rub over all the larded meat. Sauté the onion in a tablespoon of the butter and lay on the bottom of a roasting pan with the meat on top. Add the vinegar to the pan and baste the meat with the remaining butter, melted. Roast in a preheated oven at 350° for about an hour. Then sprinkle the lard with flour and baste with butter. Cook until the lard is crispy.

Julienne the lemon rind and blanch for 5 minutes in boiling water. Combine with the juices from the roast pan and serve on top of the sliced meat.

POTATOES AND PORCINI

- 2 oz. dried wild mushrooms (morels or porcini are best)
- ½ cup heavy cream
- 1 small garlic clove, minced
- 3 tbsp. unsalted butter
- 2 lbs. boiling potatoes
- Salt and pepper

Soak in warm water for 15 minutes and then rinse the reconstituted mushrooms quickly in cold water using a strainer so any grit will be removed. Chop coarsely and put in a saucepan with the heavy cream. Simmer very slowly until the cream is reduced to ¼ cup and aromatic with the mushrooms. Sauté the garlic in 1 tablespoon of the butter for a moment and add it to the mushroom/cream mixture. Season with salt and pepper and set aside. Peel the potatoes and slice them into ¼-inch slices. Rinse them twice in cold water letting them sit 10 to 15 minutes each time. Strain and dry potatoes. Butter a low earthenware-type casserole. Put in one layer of potatoes and then one layer of mushroom mixture. Make the last layer potatoes and dot with remaining butter. Season with salt and pepper and bake 30 to 40 minutes in a 425° oven.

BRAISED FENNEL

- 4 heads fennel
- 4 tbsp. unsalted butter, plus enough to butter the pan and parchment
- 1 cup stock
- Salt and pepper
- ½ cup gruyere cheese, grated

Trim, core and cut in half the four fennel heads. Butter a baking dish and arrange the fennel in it. Add 4 tablespoons of butter, stock, salt, and pepper and cover with buttered parchment paper. Cook in a preheated oven at 400° for 30 minutes. Remove the paper and continue cooking for 10 minutes. The stock should have reduced some. Now add the cheese and cook until it is melted and brown.

CLAFOUTIS

- ¾ cup milk
- ½ cup flour
- 1 tsp. vanilla (or grated lemon or orange rind)
- Pinch of salt
- 2 eggs
- ¼ cup granulated sugar
- 1 lb. cherries, pitted (or use any good fruit)
- Confectioners' sugar

Mix the milk, flour, vanilla or rind, salt, eggs and 2 tablespoons of the granulated sugar together. Butter an oven-proof serving dish and pour a third of the batter in it. Bake that for 10 minutes at 375°. Remove from the oven and add the fruit and sprinkle with the remaining sugar. Pour in the rest of the batter and continue cooking in the oven for 30 minutes. Sprinkle with confectioners' sugar and cut into pie-shaped wedges.

Venison Strip Steaks
Fried Potato Skins
Grilled Red Pepper Salad
Strawberry Ice Cream

Serves four

One of the issues with writing a game cookbook is that occasionally both the highly descriptive or rigidly precise instructions simply do not adequately convey how to accomplish the intended results. Such is the case when trying to communicate "doneness" of meat. Cooking time is always an approximate in cookbooks, especially when game is concerned, and should not be taken as the gospel. Try pressing the meat to see if it has a springy touch to it; then it's done. Wiggle a leg to see if it's loose; then it's done. Or cut into it if you're uncertain (better a slice in it than to serve it too rare or over-cooked). Enviable is a knowledgeable chef's ability to smell doneness. Experience and calling on all of your five senses to determine doneness are a more reliable guide in deciding if dinner is ready than what is printed in these pages, as much as I hate to admit it. We have put cooking times in only as a general guide on how long to gauge the cocktail hour. But always check for doneness as the cooking process progresses.

VENISON STRIP STEAKS

- 4 thin strip steaks (about ⅓ to ½ lb. each)
- 2 tbsp. oil
- ¼ cup cognac
- ½ cup veal stock
- 4 tbsp. unsalted butter
- 16 capers, large ones, loosely packed in brine
   Salt and pepper

Pan fry the steaks in oil a minute or two on each side or until done and remove to a plate. Deglaze the pan with cognac and add the stock. Reduce the liquid to ¼ cup liquid and whisk in the butter. Rinse the capers well and add to the sauce. Slice the steak, pour the juices into the sauce and season with salt and pepper. Pour the sauce over the meat.

FRIED POTATO SKINS

5 potatoes
3-5 tbsp. unsalted butter
½ garlic clove, chopped (optional)
1 tsp. parsley, chopped fine
Salt

Peel the skin off the potatoes using a potato peeler or a knife if you wish to retain more of the potato. Fry in the hot butter and garlic until crisp. Add more butter if needed. Sprinkle with the chopped parsley and sprinkle with salt.

GRILLED RED PEPPER SALAD

2-3 red peppers
2 cloves garlic, peeled
1 cup good green olive oil
Baby spinach leaves or lettuce, washed
Vinaigrette

Halve the red peppers and take out the seeds. Place them cut-side down on a piece of foil in the broiler and broil them 2 to 3 minutes till they are black. Remove and let cool. Peel the black skin off, remove any seeds and slice the peppers into pieces. Put in a jar with the garlic cloves and olive oil and let stand at least overnight. Toss with lettuce and your favorite vinaigrette. They are good in sandwiches and will last a week.

STRAWBERRY ICE CREAM

  4 egg yolks
½ cup sugar
     Pinch of salt
1½ cups medium cream
  2 tsp. framboise or vanilla extract
  6 cups berries (your ice cream will only taste as good as the berries used)
     (Enough ice and salt for the ice cream machine)

Beat together the egg yolks, sugar, and salt till they are smooth but do not ribbon. Add 1 cup cream and mix well. Put over a medium heat stirring constantly until the custard thickens. Remove from the heat, strain and whisk till cool. Add framboise or vanilla and chill. Purée the strawberries. Blend with the custard and add the remaining ½ cup of cream. Churn in ice cream machine according to the manufacturer's directions. Serve with fresh strawberries on top.

Venison Stew
Homemade Pasta
Crusted Blueberry and Cream Cake

Serves four

One of the common bonds between those who cook and those who hunt is that both avocations lead to the accumulation of equipment. It is so nice to have exactly the right little tool to accomplish the task either in the field or in the kitchen. It also could send you to the poorhouse. It is very nice indeed to own an electric pasta machine, but it is not necessary to making very good homemade pasta. It is very nice to own a choice of three deer rifles, but you can only hunt with one at a time. Use what you already own and upgrade when you know your passions.

VENISON STEW

- 2 cups red wine
- ½ cup vinegar
- 1 onion, sliced
- 1 carrot, sliced
- A few parsley stems
- 8 juniper berries
- 1 tbsp. salt
- 1 bay leaf
- 2 crushed cloves
- 4 sprigs tarragon
- 3-4 lbs. venison stew meat
- 4 tbsp. unsalted butter
- ¼ lb. pancetta, diced
- 1½ cup stock (about)
- 1 tbsp. cornstarch
- Salt and pepper

Make a marinade out of the wine, vinegar, onion, carrot, parsley stems, juniper berries, salt, bay leaf, cloves and tarragon sprigs and let the cubed venison sit in it at least overnight.

Drain the marinade from the meat and reserve it. Dry and brown the meat in butter and diced pancetta then cover by ⅔ with the marinade and stock. Cover first with foil pressed close to the meat and bringing it over the sides of the pot. And then add a lid and simmer for about an hour. Test for doneness with a skewer. Remove the meat to a bowl and strain the liquid, discarding the bay leaf, and thicken with cornstarch. Season with salt and pepper and the liquid to the pan and reheat with the meat. Serve.

HOMEMADE PASTA

- 1½ cups semolina
- 2 eggs
- All-purpose flour for dusting
- Salt
- Couple of drops of olive oil for the boiling water
- 2 tbsp. unsalted butter, melted

Make a mountain of the semolina on the counter-top and then make a crater in the mountain. Lightly beat the eggs together and pour into the crater. With a fork bring the semolina into the egg mixture slowly until all the semolina is moist, then form into two small balls. If the dough is at all sticky, add more semolina—the dough needs to be very dry. Knead for 10-20 minutes and then shape into two 8-inch-long (or so) snakes. Cut each snake into 6 pieces. Take one of the pieces and knead it for a few minutes. Flatten with the palm of your hand until it is thin enough to crank through the pasta machine on the thickest setting (#1 on the classic machine). Fold the pasta and crank through again. Repeat this two more times on this setting. Now put the pasta sheet through each progressive setting on the machine without folding it until the pasta sheet is the desired thickness. For me, this is usually after the second to the last setting (#5). Finally cut the pasta and lay on a floured cutting board and sprinkle with all-purpose flour. Toss pasta with your fingers so it is well dusted with the flour. Repeat the procedure for the remaining pieces of dough. The pasta may now be left to dry.

Of course dried pasta can be stored or cooked immediately. Fresh pasta cooks very quickly in boiling water—be sure to add salt to the water and a drop of oil—only about 2 to 3 minutes. Drain and toss with melted butter or reduced cream.

CRUSTED BLUEBERRY AND CREAM CAKE

For the cake:
- 1 quart blueberries
- 1⅓ cups all-purpose flour
- 1 tsp. dry yeast
- Pinch of salt
- 4 eggs
- ¾ cup sugar
- 1 tsp. vanilla

For the syrup:
- 1⅓ cups sugar
- ¼ cup water
- 2 tbsp. Grand Marnier
- ⅓ cup boiling water
- Whipped cream

Butter a 10-inch spring-form pan and cut a round of parchment paper to fit the bottom. Butter the paper, too, and dust both with flour.

Rinse the blueberries. Set aside.

Sift together the flour, yeast, and salt. (If need be, pulverize the yeast in a mortar before sifting.)

Over a very gentle heat, whisk eggs and sugar until quite warm, but don't allow the eggs to set around the edges. Place the eggs/sugar mixture and vanilla in a large metal mixer bowl. Continue beating by machine until the mixture mounts to a thick, almost white foam that forms a ribbon and has at least tripled in volume. Place a dense but single layer of blueberries into the spring-form pan. Pour on half the batter, sprinkle on remaining berries and cover with the rest of the batter. Bake in a preheated oven at 350° for 40 minutes.

Prepare a caramel syrup. Place 1 cup sugar and ¼ cup water in a small heavy pan over medium heat. Stir just until the sugar is dissolved, then leave alone. Let the sugar gently bubble until it starts to turn first to straw, then to deeper shades of yellow and gold and then finally to amber. Remove from heat and cool slightly. Add liqueur and ⅓ cup boiling water to make a pourable syrup.

Test cake for "doneness" by inserting a knife in the center. It should come out clean. Unmold on a serving platter and pour warm caramel syrup over the blueberried top. Sprinkle a layer of granulated sugar (about ⅓ cup) evenly over the cake and place briefly under a broiler until the sugar crystallizes into a crisp topping. Serve with whipping cream.

Venison Stew with Artichoke Hearts and Sun-dried Tomatoes
Basil Bread
Green Salad
Custard Oranges

Serves four

One year we were made a present of 50 pounds of venison, already butchered, wrapped and frozen. We didn't know the hunters or the outfitter or the butcher or even from what part of the world the deer came from. It was the first time I realized how valuable it is to be able to listen to the long, drawn-out tales of how the buck got bagged and dragged before you have to go in the kitchen and cook it. Previously, I'd always had the privilege of staring glassy-eyed at the hunter while my subconscious soaked up the pertinent details of how big and old the deer was, how clean was the shot, and what type of terrain the deer lived in. And I had been rather mechanical in applying that knowledge to my choice of recipes for the meat (see Chapter on "Game Care," 229). I learned my lesson; I certainly had a hard time figuring out what to do with those 50 pounds of meat to make them taste decent. If you can't be there yourself, at least ask a lot of questions.

The following is a recipe I would use on good quality stew meat, either a neck roast from a large deer or the shank roast from a smaller deer, cut up.

VENISON STEW WITH ARTICHOKE HEARTS AND SUN-DRIED TOMATOES

1½ lbs. venison stew meat
4 tbsp. oil
1 small onion
1 small carrot
3 cups good red wine
1 cup stock
Bouquet garni
½ cup sun-dried tomatoes
2 14 oz. cans (or two boxes frozen) artichoke hearts
1 tbsp. cornstarch
6 tbsp. butter
Salt and pepper
1 tbsp. chopped parsley
1 tbsp. grated lemon rind
1 small garlic clove, chopped fine

Brown the meat in the oil and remove from the pan. Chop the onion and carrot and sauté in the pan where the meat was. Return the meat and add the wine and stock to the pot. Bring to a boil and add the bouquet garni and sun-dried tomatoes. Soak the canned artichoke hearts for a while in cold water to remove the brine taste (this is unnecessary if they are frozen) and then add them to the pot. Cover the pan with foil, pressing down so there is no space between the foil and liquid. Put the lid on and simmer for about 20 minutes or until a skewer comes out easily and cleanly from a piece of the meat. When done, drain the juices into a frying pan and thicken with cornstarch. Whisk in the butter and season with salt and pepper. Return the meat and add the parsley, garlic and lemon rind. Check for seasoning and serve.

BASIL BREAD

    2 cups lukewarm to warm water
    1 tbsp. dry yeast
    1 tbsp. sugar
    1 tbsp. salt
    2 tbsp. dried basil
    5 cups or so of all-purpose flour (I recommend King Arthur Flour)
    Butter and oil for greasing pans

In the bowl of a standing mix master, fitted with a bread hook, add the warm water and sprinkle in the yeast, sugar, salt, and basil. Let sit for a few minutes until the yeast looks dissolved and foamy. Now pour in 5 cups of flour and mix at the lowest setting, usually marked "stir," until the flour is blended and then increase the speed to the next level, #2. Continue blending at this speed until the dough is well mixed, pulling away from the sides of the bowl, and forming a ball. Turn onto a floured surface and knead the dough for about 8 minutes. It should be slightly tacky to the touch but smooth and very malleable. Place in a bowl that has been oiled, turn the dough over in the oil so the top is oiled, too, and cover the bowl with a cloth. Let rise until it is double in size, about 2 to 3 hours. Punch it down and let it rest while you prepare the pan(s) for it to rise in again.

This recipe makes enough for a baguette and a loaf. I always make a baguette for the week's spaghetti night so I pull a handful of dough off and roll it into a big snake and lay it in one side of a baguette pan that has been buttered. The remaining dough I either place into a buttered loaf pan, pushing it into the rectangle shape, or form a ball with the dough, flouring it heavily, and put into a banneton, also heavily floured. Both the baguette and the loaf/round I cover with a cloth and let rise again for another hour or so.

The breads in the metal baking pans can go directly into a preheated oven at 420° for 35 to 40 minutes until golden brown. The banneton is trickier. I use a piece of parchment paper, floured, atop the back of a cookie sheet and careful invert the banneton and let the dough fall out. Often it loses its rise and I let it sit covered for another hour to rise again. Once the round is ready to bake I slide it onto a pizza stone that is in a preheated oven at 420º and bake it for 40 minutes or until golden. Once baked, I turn the baguette and loaf out of their pans—or slide the round on the parchment onto the cookie sheet—and onto a rack to cool. Let cool for 30 minutes or so before cutting.

If I don't plan to use the baguette that day I wrap it in foil and put it in the freezer to use another day. (It just needs to be taken from the freezer and put in a preheated oven at 350º for 30 minutes or so.)

CUSTARD ORANGES

4 large navel oranges
3 egg yolks
⅓ cup sugar
1½ oz. Cointreau
1⅓ cup heavy cream

Cut off the top of each orange and scoop out the inside. Rinse and let drain. Beat the egg yolks and sugar together then add the Cointreau. Now whip 1 cup of the cream until it is stiff. Stir in ⅓ of the whipped cream and then fold in the rest of the whipped cream. Fill each orange with the egg-cream mixture and set on a plate in the refrigerator for at least two hours. When ready to serve whip the remaining ⅓ cup cream and put a dollop on each orange top. Dust with cocoa.

Venison with Port
Roast Potatoes
Sautéed Watercress
Meyer Lemon Sherbet

Serves four

VENISON WITH PORT

        Pork lard (enough to cover the saddle in 2-inch strips)
- 4-5 lbs. saddle of venison (see page 36)
- 4 carrots
- 4 onions
- A few parsley stems
- ⅔ cup unsalted butter
- 2 cups port
- ½ tsp. powdered cloves
- ½ tsp. cinnamon

Preheat the oven to 500°. Lard the saddle and tie with string to hold in place. Peel and chop fine the carrots, onions and parsley stems. Sauté them all in 6 tablespoons of the butter. Lay the vegetables on the bottom of a roasting pan and put the venison on top. Pour the port over it and cook for about 10 minutes. Lower the heat to 400° and continue to cook for another half hour or so basting every 10 minutes. Remove the meat from the pan, skim off any fat and, on top of the stove, reduce the liquid that's left to about half a cup. Add the clove and cinnamon and whisk in the remaining butter and juices which might have exuded from the sliced meat. Check for salt and pepper and serve over slices of the meat.

SAUTÉED WATERCRESS

    3 bunches of watercress, washed and spun dry
  3-4 tbsp. unsalted butter
      Salt and pepper

Take each bunch of watercress and cut into 2-inch lengths (the bunches should be cut approximately into thirds). Sauté the watercress in the hot unsalted butter for a second or two then put on the lid for two minutes. Remove the lid, season with salt and pepper and a little more butter, and serve.

MEYER LEMON SHERBET

  7-8 Meyer lemons (to make 1 cup of juice)
  1½ cups sugar
  1½ cups water
    1 tbsp. at least Meyer lemon rind, slivered and chopped fine
   ¾ cup whole milk
    2 tbsp. water
    1 tsp. gelatin
      (Enough kosher salt and ice cubes for your ice cream machine)

Juice the Meyer lemons, making sure you have a full cup, and reserve the rind from one of the lemons. In a small saucepan combine the sugar and water and heat until the sugar is completely dissolved. Sliver the lemon rind and chop fine. In a bowl, pour the sugar water and the lemon juice and add in the milk and lemon rind. In the saucepan put the 2 tablespoons of water and stir in the gelatin and let it sit until the gelatin has plumped up-about a minute or two. Then heat it gently so there is no graininess. Stir in the gelatin now to the lemon-milk mixture, cover the bowl with plastic wrap, and refrigerate for at least six hours until it is very cold. Then freeze it according to the instructions with your ice cream maker.

Venison Scallops
Persillade Potatoes
Green Beans
Tarte Tatin

Serves four

VENISON SCALLOPS

- 2 tbsp. coarsely chopped hazelnuts
- 3 tbsp. oil
- Rind from one quarter of an orange
- 8-10 venison scallops (slice ½-inch pieces of meat from a good cut of roast, like the eye of the round, making sure to cut across the grain).
- ¼ cup Armagnac
- 1 cup stock
- ¼ cup plus 1 tbsp. unsalted butter
- Salt and pepper

Toast the nuts in the oven till they are light brown. Wrap in a towel for 10 minutes to create steam and to loosen the skin from the nut, rub off the skins and sauté in 1 tablespoon oil. Chop fine.

Remove the orange rind (making sure to get no pith) from the orange with a potato peeler and julienne into slivers. Blanch for 5 minutes in boiling water. Rinse, drain and reserve.

Pan fry the scalloped venison in 2 tablespoons of oil for a minute or two on each side. Remove from the pan and set aside. Deglaze the pan with Armagnac and then add the stock and reduce the liquid to ¼ cup. Whisk in the butter and season with salt and pepper. Add the nuts and orange slivers and serve over the venison scallops.

PERSILLADE POTATOES

- 2 garlic cloves
- ½ bunch parsley
- 2 large potatoes
- 2 tbsp. bacon fat or butter
- Salt and pepper

Chop the garlic and parsley fine and mix together. Peel and slice the potatoes very thin and then sauté them in bacon fat over a medium heat with the lid on for five minutes. Remove the lid and add the parsley and garlic mixture and cook for a few more minutes. Season with salt and pepper and serve.

TARTE TATIN

- 6 hard cooking apples (uncommon apples like Calville Blanc d'Hiver or Esopus Spitzenberg are my favorite for this recipe, but Baldwins or Cortlands work too)
- ¾ cup sugar, plus a sprinkle
- ½ cup water
- 2 tbsp. unsalted butter
- Sprinkle of cinnamon
- 1 sheet Pepperidge Farm Puff Pastry, or your own pastry
- Lightly whipped cream

Peel and slice the apples thinly. Next caramelize the sugar by cooking the water and ¾ cup sugar in a frying pan until it is light brown. Remove immediately from the heat as it will continue to cook and transfer to a cake tin. Spread the caramelized sugar over the bottom and lay the apple slices in concentric circles on top. Only the first layer will show so be sure to make that your best. Dot each layer with butter and sprinkle with sugar and cinnamon. Once the pan is full roll out the pastry and cover the apples with it. Cut a few tiny holes in the pastry to let the steam escape. Cook in the middle of a preheated oven at 450° for 20 minutes. Then turn the heat down to 350° and continue to cook for 30 to 40 minutes. Remove and let cool for a few minutes and then invert onto a serving plate. If it has hardened too much, put the cake tin on a burner and re-melt the caramel. Then invert.

You can add a bit of the extra juices that may run out, once cooled, to the lightly whipped cream.

Venison Chops with Pignolis and Red Peppers
Pepperoni Bread
Green Salad
Stuffed Oranges

Serves four

When I was a child, unsalted butter made me lose my appetite; it simply did not seem right. As an adult I never use salted butter. Of course, historically salt was added to butter to mask any rancidity. And from what I can tell that is still the only reason for adding it to butter, save some lurking childhood biases. Unsalted butter can be more expensive but can be easily justified by treating it as a healthier alternative. Who needs more salt in their diet?

VENISON CHOPS WITH PIGNOLIS AND RED PEPPERS

1 sweet red pepper
2 tbsp. unsalted butter
¼ cup pignolis (pine nuts)
¼ cup walnut oil
4 venison chops
   Salt and pepper

Cut the red pepper and take the seeds out. Slice into thin strips and sauté in the butter. Sauté the pignolis nuts separately in 2 tablespoons of the walnut oil. Toss the peppers and nuts together and set aside.

Sauté the chops in the remaining walnut oil for a minute or two on each side. Place on plates and add the pepper and nut mixture to the top of each chop. Season with salt and pepper to taste.

PEPPERONI BREAD

2 cups lukewarm to warm water
1 tbsp. dry yeast
1 tbsp. sugar
1 tbsp. salt

5 cups all-purpose flour
⅔ cup pepperoni, chopped
Butter or oil for greasing pans

In the bowl of a standing mix master, fitted with a bread hook, add the warm water and sprinkle in the yeast, sugar, and salt. Let sit for a few minutes until the yeast looks dissolved and foamy. Now pour in 5 cups of flour and mix at the lowest setting, usually marked "stir," until the flour is blended and then increase the speed to the next level, #2. Continue blending at this speed until the dough is well mixed, pulling away from the sides of the bowl, and forming a ball. Add the chopped pepperoni to the dough. Turn onto a floured surface and knead the dough for about 8 minutes. It should be slightly tacky to the touch but smooth and very malleable. Place in a bowl that has been oiled, turn the dough over in the oil so the top is oiled, too, and cover the bowl with a cloth. Let rise until it is double in size, about 2 to 3 hours. Punch it down and let it rest while you prepare the pan(s) for it to rise in again.

This recipe makes enough for a baguette and a loaf. I always make a baguette for the week's spaghetti night so I pull a handful of dough off and roll it into a big snake and lay it in one side of a baguette pan that has been buttered. The remaining dough I used to make the Pepperoni bread for this menu by forming a ball with the dough, flouring it heavily, and putting it into a banneton, also heavily floured. Both the baguette and the round I cover with a cloth and let rise again for another hour or so.

Using a banneton can be a bit tricky but it produces a beautiful round of bread. Using a piece of parchment paper, floured, atop the back of a cookie sheet, I carefully invert the banneton and let the dough fall out. Often it loses its rise and I let it sit covered for another hour to rise again. Once the round is ready to bake I slide it onto a pizza stone that is in a preheated oven at 420° and bake it and the baguette for 35 to 40 minutes or until golden. Once baked, I turn the baguette out onto a cooling rack and slide the round on the parchment onto the cookie sheet—and also onto the rack to cool. Let cool for 30 minutes or so before cutting.

If I don't plan to use the baguette that day I wrap it in foil and put it in the freezer to use another day. (It just needs to be taken from the freezer and put in a preheated oven at 350° for 30 minutes or so.) .

STUFFED ORANGES

    4 large navel oranges
    1 qt. orange ice or sherbet
       Sprigs of mint

Cut off the top of each orange and scoop out the orange and pith inside. Rinse and let drain. Soften the sherbet or ice and then fill each orange shell. Refreeze and then decorate with sprigs of mint.

Venison Chops with Mustard Butter
Roast Potatoes with Rosemary
Green Beans and Beet Salad
Coffee Granita

Serves four

In many of the recipes I have listed veal stock as an ingredient. Veal stock is not something that can be easily bought—even my old standby game purveyor, D'Artagnan, who always has everything, lists only a duck and veal demi-glace and is out of stock a lot. Although expensive and time-consuming, it is not difficult to make and is very, very worth doing. For many great cooks, it's a once-a-month ritual, and the 12-hour simmer can even take place while you sleep. After it has become a part of your life it will be like hunting: The extra time and effort is simply not remembered, only how good it is. (see page 64)

VENISON CHOPS WITH MUSTARD BUTTER

- 4 venison chops
- 1 tbsp. oil
- ¼ cup cognac
- ¼ cup veal stock
- ½ cup heavy cream
- 1 tbsp. prepared course-grained mustard
- Salt and pepper

Pan fry the chops in oil and set aside. Deglaze the pan with cognac and add the veal stock and cream. Reduce to half the quantity, remove from heat, and whisk in any juices that have oozed from the resting chops. Add the mustard. Season to taste with salt and pepper and serve over the chops.

ROAST POTATOES WITH ROSEMARY

  16 little red potatoes
   4 tbsp. melted, unsalted butter
       Rosemary
       Salt and pepper

Paint the potatoes with the melted butter and sprinkle liberally with rosemary. Roast in the oven for about 45 minutes at 350° or until they are tender. Season with salt and pepper.

GREEN BEANS AND BEET SALAD

   1 lb. green beans
   8 medium-size beets
   1 tbsp. vinegar
   1 tsp. prepared mustard
  ½ cup olive or walnut oil
      Splash of soy sauce
      Salt and pepper
      Lettuce
      Mint

Blanch the beans in salted boiling water until they are just tender. Plunge them into ice water to stop the cooking and preserve the color. Drain them and let dry. Steam the beets until they are tender and can be pierced with a fork (about half an hour). Let them cool, peel and julienne them. Make a vinaigrette by combining in a blender the vinegar, mustard, oil, soy sauce, salt and pepper. Pour half the vinaigrette on the beets and half on the beans and toss each separately, as the beets will bleed if you toss them too much together. Then toss the two vegetables together gently and serve on a bed of lettuce with a sprig of mint on each serving.

COFFEE GRANITA

  1½ cups strong espresso coffee (Italian roasted)
   2 tbsp. sugar
      Heavy cream

If the coffee is not strong enough let it infuse with the grounds for ½ hour or so. Then strain. Dissolve the sugar in the coffee and chill. Then freeze in ice trays or a brownie tin, stirring every 15 minutes or so for about 3 hours. Serve immediately with cream or whipped cream. Coffee Granita is not meant to be a solid ice. It should be melt-in-your-mouth texture.

Venison Steak with Wild Mushrooms
Blue Cheese Polenta
Spinach and Bibb Lettuce Salad
Strawberry Ice

Serves four

For many years I worked on the food photography for *Gray's Sporting Journal* and then later on the food photography for several of my books. The process always focused on how to achieve the most attractive food presentation. What the eye perceives as being luscious becomes so to the taste buds, too. It is an art, and although published food photos are labored over by professional photographers and stylists, I have seen equal creativity in the practiced cook. Game, of course, can present its own unique problems for pleasant presentation at the table. But the extra moments spent pulling every feather from the duck legs or taking a pair of tweezers to the venison to remove the last hair is worth more to the assurance of a tasty meal than any exotic recipe.

VENISON STEAK WITH WILD MUSHROOMS

- 1 oz. dried wild mushrooms
- 1 cup cream
- 2 lbs. venison steak
- 1 tbsp. oil
- ¼ cup cognac or Armagnac
- ⅓ cup veal stock
- Salt and pepper

Soak the mushrooms in warm water for about 15 minutes and then rinse and put into a sauté pan with the cream. Bring it to a boil and then turn it down to a slow simmer. Continue to simmer until the cream is reduced by half.

Pan fry the steak in the oil and remove to a plate to let rest. Deglaze the pan with cognac and add the veal stock. Bring to a boil and let reduce by half. Add the cream and mushroom mixture and any juices that have exuded from the resting steak and let simmer together for a few minutes. Season with salt and pepper and serve over the sliced meat.

BLUE CHEESE POLENTA

- 1 small onion (optional)
- 6 tbsp. unsalted butter
- 2 cups milk
- ¾ cup cornmeal
- 5 oz. blue cheese, diced
- ½ tsp. nutmeg
- 2 tsp. kosher salt
- ½ cup heavy cream
- Pepper

If you are using the onion, sauté it in 2 tablespoons of the butter until translucent. Then, in a small saucepan bring the onion, remaining butter, and milk to a boil. Add the cornmeal slowly, stirring constantly till thick and the spoon can stand up in it. Be careful as the polenta will spit at you. Now add the cheese, nutmeg and salt. Remove from the heat and beat in the cream and pepper. Turn immediately into buttered muffin tins and let rest till set. Remove from the tin and put in a heavy oven-proof pan and cook at 400° for 15 minutes. (If you like, you can add a little more cheese to the tops of the polenta muffins before putting them in the oven.)

STRAWBERRY ICE

- 6 cups strawberries (approximately)
- 1 cup sugar
- Pinch of salt and a squirt of lemon juice if needed
- 1 tbsp. Kirsch
- (Remember to have enough ice and salt for your ice cream freezer, too.)

Wash and hull the strawberries. Purée in the blender. You should have about 1 quart of purée. Boil half a cup of water and add the sugar and cook for 5 minutes. Let cool. Add the sugar syrup to the fruit juice as needed to please your taste. Add salt and lemon juice to help the taste if need be and then pour in the Kirsch. Chill the mixture in the canister from your ice cream maker. Then freeze according to the ice cream machine's directions.

Venison Steaks Marinated
Grilled Red Pepper Salad
Mashed Potatoes with Fresh Basil
Vanilla Ice Cream with Homemade Butterscotch Sauce

Serves four

Twenty-five years ago when I first wrote this book I was careful, where applicable, to always include: "remove the bay leaf" in the instructions. Of course, every cookbook instructs bay leaf removal before serving and I wondered why? Back then when I questioned my cooking teacher, she said that bay leaves are not digested and their sharp edges can actually perforate the stomach wall. Now older and less intimidated by a cooking professional, I decided this sounded perhaps a bit over the top and did a little Wikipedia research. I found nothing about perforated stomachs but rather "the oft-repeated belief that bay leaves should be removed from food after cooking because they are poisonous. This is not true—bay leaves are safe to eat. However, they remain very stiff even after thorough cooking, and because of this, they are not considered culinarily acceptable, and could even pose a potential choking hazard." Whether it's a problem with a perforated stomach or potential for choking, better take that bay leaf out!

VENISON STEAKS MARINATED

- 25-30 juniper berries, lightly toasted and crushed
- Lemon zest from 2 lemons
- 1 tsp. celery salt
- 10 peppercorns, crushed
- 2 tbsp. ground coriander seed
- 1 bay leaf, crumbled
- 2½ cups olive oil
- Juice from 2 lemons (about ⅓ cup)
- 2 lbs. venison steak
- 2 tbsp. unsalted butter
- ¼ cup cognac
- ⅔ cup veal stock
- ½ cup heavy cream
- 2 tsp. sour cream
- Salt and pepper

In a blender, or with a mortar and pestle, blend the juniper berries, lemon rind, celery salt, peppercorns, and coriander seed. Add this to the oil, bay leaf, and lemon juice and marinate the steak overnight.

Wipe the steak dry and pan fry it in butter. Remove the meat and let rest. Deglaze the pan with cognac and then add the veal stock. Bring to a boil and reduce ¼ of the liquid. Add the heavy cream and continue to let it boil and reduce. Add any juices that have exuded from the steak while it has been resting and after it has been carved. Remove the sauce from the heat and whisk in salt and pepper and the sour cream. Serve over the steak.

VEAL STOCK

- 6 lbs. veal shank
- 3 lbs. veal trimmings
- 3 lbs. veal bones
- 4 large onions, not peeled, with a clove stuck in one
- 3-4 carrots, peeled
- 3 cups white wine
- 2 tsp. salt
- Peppercorns
- Parsley Stems
- Bay leaf
- Thyme

In the oven and in several batches, brown the meat. It is best to do in a large roasting pan. Don't let the bottom burn. Add a little water if necessary as you go along.

Put all meat in a large stock pot. Add the bones, onions, and carrots.

In the roasting pan where the meat was browned add water and wine to cover the dried meat juices to a level of about 1 inch. Bring this to a boil on top of the stove scraping the sides and bottom with a whisk. When the juice is just a ½-inch layer on the bottom of the pan add it to the stock pot with the meat and vegetables.

Fill the rest of the pot with water to cover the meat and vegetables.

Bring to a boil and then turn down to a simmer. Add 2 teaspoons of salt, several peppercorns, parsley stems, bay leaf, and thyme.

Cook 12 hours adding boiling water as necessary to keep the stock level up. Strain through a colander lined with a wet piece of cheesecloth. Skim off the fat and cook down to ⅓ in quantity and let cool again to room temperature. Freeze in ice cube trays. Once frozen remove with a knife and store cubes in plastic bags.

Do not let the stock sit long at room temperature or it will sour. And never let it sit at room temperature with the bones in; always strain them out even if you have to stop the cooking in the middle, only to restart later. Meat stock is fertile ground for bacteria.

GRILLED RED PEPPER SALAD

    2-3 red peppers
      2 cloves garlic, peeled
      1 cup good green olive oil

Halve the red peppers and take out the seeds (or use whole). Place them cut-side down on a piece of foil in the broiler and broil them 2 to 3 minutes till they are black. Remove and let cool. Peel the black skin off, remove the seeds and slice the peppers into pieces. Put in a jar with the garlic cloves and olive oil and let stand at least over night. Toss with lettuce and your favorite vinaigrette. These are good in sandwiches, too.

MASHED POTATOES WITH FRESH BASIL

    4 medium-size potatoes (russet)
    ½ cup (1 stick) unsalted butter, softened and cut
        into pats
    ½ cup or so of the reserved cooking water
        Fresh basil to taste
        Salt and pepper to taste

Wash, peel, and quarter the potatoes. Put the potatoes in cold salted water and bring them to a boil and cook till they are soft when you insert a fork, about 20 minutes. Remove them from the water, reserving half a cup, and push the potatoes through a sieve or potato ricer into a bowl. Add the butter and reserved water and whisk till fluffy. Chop the basil and add it with the salt and pepper to the potatoes and taste.

If you are trying to hold the potatoes, put them in a double boiler, uncovered, and save half of the butter and water to add at the last minute.

HOMEMADE BUTTERSCOTCH

  2 cups sugar
 ¾ cups water
     Pinch of salt
2½ cups hot cream
  4 tbsp. unsalted butter (optional)

Make a sugar syrup with the sugar, water, and salt. Cook till light brown. Remove from heat and add the heated cream stirring all the time. For a richer sauce, add the softened butter after the cream.

Grilled Venison Steak with Rosemary Butter
Bibb Lettuce and Tomato Salad
White Bean Purée
Coffee Ice Cream with Hazelnut Liqueur

Serves four

In beef the cut of meat identifies for us the quality of the meat. Unfortunately what we have learned is a great cut of beef is not necessarily paralleled in venison. Venison steaks, for example, are quite often the less desirable cut of meat; the chops the best. Nonetheless, you can't go wrong with a grilled steak.

GRILLED VENISON STEAK WITH ROSEMARY BUTTER

- 2 tsp. dried rosemary
- ½ tsp. garlic, chopped
- ½ cup (1 stick) unsalted butter
- Salt and pepper
- 2 lbs. venison steak

Chop the rosemary and the garlic very fine. Whip the butter and add the rosemary, garlic and salt and pepper to taste. Wrap the butter in plastic wrap and shape into a log. Place in the freezer while you start the charcoal or heat up the gas grill. Once the grill is very hot, cook the steak quickly. Cut slices of the butter to go on top of each serving.

WHITE BEAN PURÉE

  1 lb. white beans, soaked an hour
2½ cups chicken stock
2½ cups water
  1 onion
  2 cloves
  1 bay leaf
     Pinch of thyme
     A few parsley stems
     Salt and pepper
¾ cup heavy cream
½ cup (1 stick) unsalted butter, softened

Drain the soaking beans and pour in the water and broth (if you don't have any chicken stock, all water with chicken bouillon cubes is fine). Peel the onion and push the cloves into it. Add the onion, bay leaf, thyme, parsley stems and salt and pepper to the bean pot and bring to a boil. Simmer until the beans are tender (about a half hour to an hour). Remove bay leaf. In small batches, churn up the bean mixture in a food processor. Zipping it for just a second not to purée, but just to break the skins of the beans. Push through a strainer back into the pot and mix in the cream and butter. Reheat gently and season with salt and pepper.

Venison Chops with Blue Cheese and Caraway Seeds
Sweet Potato Gratin
Braised Fennel
Fresh Figs

Serves four

VENISON CHOPS WITH BLUE CHEESE AND CARAWAY SEEDS

- ½ cup (1 stick) unsalted butter, softened
- 1 tbsp. blue cheese, crumbled
- ½ tsp. crushed caraway seeds
- Few drops of Worcestershire sauce
- Pepper to taste
- 4 chops
- 2½ tbsp. oil

Whip the butter till it is fluffy. Add the cheese, caraway, Worcestershire and pepper and mix well. Roll up in plastic wrap and shape into a log and freeze for at least 1 hour or preferably overnight. Pan fry the chops in oil, about two or three minutes a side (depending on thickness) and place on plates. Slice off two or three pats of the cheese/butter per chop and put them on top to melt over the chops.

SWEET POTATO GRATIN

3	white potatoes
3	yellow sweet potatoes (or yams)
2½	cups cream
½	tsp. cognac
¼	tsp. nutmeg
¼	tsp. powdered cloves
	A pinch of thyme
	Salt and pepper
	(Butter for greasing the dish)

Peel and cut the potatoes into thin ⅛-inch slices. Layer in a buttered baking dish and add the cream, cognac, nutmeg, clove, thyme, and salt and pepper. Bake at 325° for 1½ hours.

BRAISED FENNEL

4	heads fennel
4	tbsp. unsalted butter sliced into pats
1	cup stock
	Salt and pepper
½	cup gruyere cheese, grated

Trim, core and cut in half the four fennel heads. Butter a baking dish and arrange the fennel in it. Add the pats of butter, stock, and salt and pepper and cover with buttered parchment paper. Cook in a preheated oven at 400° for 30 minutes. Remove the paper and baste the fennel, continue cooking for 10 to 20 minutes longer. The stock should have reduced somewhat. Now add the cheese and cook until it is melted and brown.

Venison Steak with Red Wine
Bittergreens and Cheese Salad
Garlic Toasts
Rhubarb Tart

Serves four

All game, because of its high protein content, continues to cook significantly after it has been removed from the heat source. But for some reason I have found it more so with venison than with other type of game. It is worth being aware of—you can always cook something more but not less. Also, not only does game continue to cook, it then loses heat very quickly and becomes cold. We make an extra effort to serve game on warmed plates or platters so it is still warm when it gets to the table.

VENISON STEAK WITH RED WINE

- 2 lbs. venison steak
- 2 tbsp. oil
- 6 tbsp. unsalted butter
- 2 tbsp. finely chopped shallots
- ⅔ cup good red wine (the better the wine, the better the sauce)
- ½ cup veal stock
- Salt and pepper

Pan fry the steak in oil until done. Remove to a platter. In the pan put one of the tablespoons of butter and the shallots over a medium heat and cook until they are just barely soft. Add the wine and bring to a boil and continue boiling until you have ⅓ left. Add the veal stock and simmer till half of that is left, you should have about ½ cup liquid in all now. Slice the meat against the grain. Whisk in the remaining butter to the sauce and any of the juices from the steak on the platter. Season with salt and pepper and serve the sauce over the steak.

BITTERGREENS AND CHEESE SALAD

    Escarole, chicory or arugula
    Bibb lettuce
4 strips of bacon
3 oz. blue cheese
    Vinaigrette

Wash and dry the lettuce and greens and break into bite-size pieces. Cut the bacon into 1-inch pieces and fry till medium done, not crisp. Cut the cheese into cubes. Combine the lettuce, bacon and cheese and toss with the vinaigrette. Serve.

GARLIC TOASTS

1 loaf French bread
8 heads of firm garlic
5 tbsp. good green olive oil
    Salt and pepper

Cut the French bread into ½-inch slices and toast on a cookie sheet in a 300° oven making sure both sides are lightly browned.

Separate all the garlic cloves, peel and remove any green sprouts. Boil all the cloves in a couple quarts of cold, salted water for 5 minutes. Drain and repeat the boiling process three more times. The garlic cloves should be easily pierced with a fork. Purée the cloves with the olive oil in a food processor or blender or mash with a fork. Add salt and pepper to taste. Spread the garlic purée on the toast and run under the broiler to glaze. Serve.

RHUBARB TART

- ½ lb. pastry (yours or a sheet of Pepperidge Farm Puff Pastry or mine, p. 250)
- 3 lbs. rhubarb (preferably the young sticks)
- ¾ cup sugar, plus enough to sprinkle on the pastry
- 1 lemon, grated
- Splash of vanilla or sherry
- ⅔ cup crème fraîche, or a mixture of sour cream and heavy cream
- 2 tbsp. confectioners' sugar
- ½ tsp. powdered cloves

Roll out the pastry into a buttered 9-inch tart or pastry dish and refrigerate for 1 hour.

With a knife peel the thin outer layer from each stick of rhubarb and slice very thinly. Put in a heavy saucepan with the granulated sugar. Cover and cook 15 minutes over a medium low heat. Then remove the lid and turn the heat up to evaporate all the juices. Stir constantly so it will not stick and burn. Once it has become the consistency of jam remove and let cool. Add the lemon rind and a few drops of the vanilla or sherry.

Prick the bottom of the refrigerated pastry shell with a fork and place foil tightly over the pastry. Fill with pie weights or beans and cook on the lower shell of a preheated oven at 425° for 8 minutes. Remove the foil and weights, prick the crust again, sprinkle with a little granulated sugar and return it to the oven for 5 more minutes or until the crust is caramelized. Remove it from the oven and carefully slide the crust onto a cake rack to cool.

Whip the cream and sour cream (or just the crème fraîche) together with the confectioners' sugar and clove. When it's thick, spread it over the bottom of the pastry shell. Then spread the rhubarb over the whipped cream mixture and serve within 30 minutes, otherwise the crust becomes soggy.

Venison Calzone
Sliced Tomatoes with Basil
Fried Sage Leaves
Poached Pears

Serves four

Deer are everywhere, it seems. I was particularly impressed with that fact after visiting friends in Connecticut. Ed was on a deer hunt and I had ventured off to a Ducks Unlimited dinner unescorted. Rather than make the trip back to Massachusetts the same evening I stayed the night with friends. In the morning the offer of a quick pass through their back woods in search of deer was made. The concept of potentially shooting a deer in Connecticut while I was on a morning stroll and with Ed in the Maine woods for a week trying to get his deer tickled my fancy. Dressed improperly in the cocktail party attire of the previous evening and allowing only an hour for the hunt (only in Connecticut could the attire or time limit even vaguely work for a deer hunt), I was amazed to get a glimpse at some 20 good-sized deer in the space of that hour. And we would have had our venison had it not been for some near-sighted shooting on the part of my companion.

As some 122,816,330 pounds of wild venison are brought to the tables in America annually, variety in recipes is mandatory. This recipe offers a good change of pace from venison loaf or burgers.

VENISON CALZONE

- 3 cups all-purpose flour
- 2¼ tsp. or 1 pkg. dry yeast
- 2 tbsp. oregano
- 1 cup ground venison
- 1 clove garlic
- Bacon fat
- 1 cup eggplant, cubed
- 1 tbsp. oil
- ½ cup slivered gruyere cheese
- ¼ cup chopped parsley
- Salt and pepper

In a medium size bowl mix 1 cup of the flour with the yeast and add enough warm water (not hot water) to make a moist and cohesive ball. Fill the bowl with warm water so the ball is covered. Let sit 5 to 15 minutes until the ball pops to the surface. Meanwhile take the remaining amount of flour (this can be all white flour or a mixture such as ⅔ white and ⅓ whole wheat) and put it on top of the counter. Make a trench in the middle of the pile and add the salt. Reconstitute the oregano by pouring a little hot water in with it first and then add it to the flour trench. You will need to add more water, as much as a cup or so, fluffing it into the flour with your fingers. The mixture should be slightly cohesive but not wet as the yeast/flour ball will be quite wet. When the ball has risen to the surface of the water, scoop it out and set in the middle of your pile of flour. Knead the ball and the flour together and continue to knead for 8 minutes or so. Put the dough in an oiled or floured bowl with a towel over it and place in a warm spot to rise two hours or until doubled in bulk. Punch down and roll out into a 6-inch by 12-inch rectangle.

Now brown the venison in the bacon fat and sauté the eggplant in the oil. Put the burger, eggplant, and grated cheese in layers in the center of the dough and sprinkle with parsley, salt, and pepper. Then pull the sides of the dough up over the meat mixture and wrap tightly, pinching the seams. Flip over so the seam is on the bottom. Let rise again and bake in a preheated oven at 425° till done (about 35-40 minutes).

FRIED SAGE LEAVES

½ cup large sage leaves
2 tbsp. unsalted butter
Salt

Fry the sage leaves in butter until they're stiff but not browned. Remove with wooden tongs and season with salt.

POACHED PEARS

4 ripe pears
Lemon juice
2 cups water
1⅓ cups sugar
1 vanilla bean, split

Peel the pears with a vegetable peeler and core from the bottom with a melon baller. Rub the peeled pears with lemon juice. In a saucepan combine water, a few drops of lemon juice, and sugar and bring it to a boil. Add the split vanilla bean and reduce the heat. Simmer for 5 minutes. Then add the pears and continue to simmer for about 10 minutes or until the pears are tender. Remove the pears from the syrup and stand upright on a plate in the refrigerator. The chilled pears can be served with crème anglaise, whipped cream, chocolate shavings, or a liqueur over it.

**Venison Chops with Basil Cream
Homemade Pasta with Parsley
Salad with Hazelnut Dressing
Brandied Apricots with Crème Anglaise**

Serves four

VENISON CHOPS WITH BASIL CREAM

- 1 pint heavy cream
- ½ tbsp. dried basil
- 4 venison chops
- 1 tbsp. oil
- 1 tbsp. unsalted butter
- Splash of veal stock or brandy to deglaze
- Salt and pepper

Reduce the cream. Pour the cream into a frying pan, bring to a slow boil and add the basil. Simmer until halved in quantity and thick. If it gets too thick add a little water and stir. Meanwhile cook the chops. Brush away any bone chips left from butchering and remove all fat from the venison. In a frying pan with the hot oil and butter, sauté the chops very quickly, 2 or 3 minutes per side. Remember venison continues to cook long after it comes off the heat. The chops should be pink. Remove the chops and in the pan add a tiny amount of stock or brandy and deglaze; then add the basil cream. Stir and season with salt and pepper and serve with the chops.

HOMEMADE PASTA WITH PARSLEY

- 1½ cups semolina
- 2 eggs
- All-purpose flour for dusting
- Salt
- Couple of drops of olive oil for the boiling water
- 2 tbsp. unsalted butter, melted
- 2 tbsp. finely chopped parsley

Make a mountain of the semolina on the counter-top and then make a crater in the mountain. Lightly beat the eggs together and pour into the crater. With a fork bring the semolina into the egg mixture slowly until all the semolina is moist, then form into two small balls. If the dough is at all sticky, add more semolina—the dough needs to be very dry. Knead for 10-20 minutes and then shape into two 8-inch-long (or so) snakes. Cut each snake into 6 pieces. Take one of the pieces and knead it for a few minutes. Flatten with the palm of your hand until it is thin enough to crank through the pasta machine on the thickest setting (#1 on the classic machine). Fold the pasta and crank through again. Repeat this two more times on this setting. Now put the pasta sheet through each progressive setting on the machine without folding it until the pasta sheet is the desired thickness. For me, this is usually after the second to the last setting (#5). Finally cut the pasta and lay on a floured cutting board and sprinkle with all-purpose flour. Toss pasta with your fingers so it is well dusted with the flour. Repeat the procedure for the remaining pieces of dough. The pasta may now be left to dry.

Of course dried pasta can be stored or cooked immediately. Freshly-made pasta cooks very quickly in boiling water—be sure to add salt to the water and a drop of oil—only about 2 to 3 minutes. Drain and toss with melted butter and parsley.

HAZELNUT SALAD

> Boston lettuce
> ½ cup toasted and crushed hazelnuts
> ¾ cup hazelnut oil
> 3 tbsp. vinegar
> 1 clove shallot, chopped fine
> 1 tsp. prepared mustard
> Salt and pepper

Wash and spin dry the lettuce. Toast the hazelnuts in the oven.

Remove and cover with a tea towel to steam. Rub the skins off the nuts and chop fine. Sprinkle over the lettuce.

Combine the remaining ingredients in the blender and zip on high for a few seconds. Pour over the salad and toss.

BRANDIED APRICOTS WITH CRÈME ANGLAISE

> 1 lb. apricots
> 3 cups brandy (or enough to cover)

Place the apricots in a jar and cover with brandy. Seal and let stand at least 48 hours. Serve with crème anglaise (see page 221).

Upland Birds

"Oh boy," my friend P.J. O'Rourke wryly remarked. "It looks like pterodactyl's for supper." We were standing in the bathroom of my motel room at the Ramkota Inn in Pierre, South Dakota, having cocktails and discussing the day's various hunting events. Feeling a bit like the Vanna White of a very different kind of game show, I was holding the shower curtain aside to reveal a large-size green garbage bag, the legs of two sandhill cranes sticking stiffly and inelegantly out the top. Not exactly dinosaurs, of course, but probably at least distant cousins and nearly as unlikely candidates for the main course of tonight's dinner. We were, however, quite committed now.

It had been an unpredictable kind of day. And frankly, the fact that I'd need to rummage through my mental scrapbook of recipes searching for a suitable sandhill crane concoction wasn't actually the first surprise. No, that had begun right off when Wicker Bill—a local, and renowned duck hunting guide—showed up pre-dawn in the rear parking lot of the motel to take Ed, our friend Kris, and me on a duck hunt. Here we were in South Dakota pheasant and sharptail shooting but able to complete our hunting potpourri with ducks. Now camouflaged and down-vested, we drank gallons of black coffee and headed out at oh-dark-thirty; and true to the western notion of distance, "out" turned out to be way out—like a couple of hours out. So when we arrived where the migrating ducks were rumored to be resting, Wicker's now greatly suppressed eagerness was clearly nearing climax. Had the truck even come to a stop before he jumped from the cab, snuck with urgency and practiced stealth—at times on his belly—to the appointed prairie pothole? As he went, he calculated, I'm sure, a most professional ambush on the unsuspecting waterfowl. Alas, the surprise was for us. There wasn't a duck to be had or likely would there be in the very near future: The pothole had been transformed into an ice rink, frozen solid.

It was getting very light and bright out now, not duck hunting conditions; but Wicker Bill was still enthusiastic, a determined kind of guy not easily deterred when it came to hunting. He proposed we go in search of sandhill crane: nearly a pest in the West, there is not only a legal hunting season on the bird but their demise is much appreciated by the farmers whose crops they ravage. We'd seen dozens of high-flying and out-of-gunshot-range flocks in our morning travels and Wicker confirmed they were difficult to shoot. Considered very sporting, he knew lots of locals that had tried for years to shoot a sandhill crane with no success. This might have been guide-speak (i.e. greatly exaggerated statement); nonetheless the gantlet was now thrown.

In Wicker's truck we raced the dirt roads, scanning the sky for flying lines of cranes, trying to anticipate where they might set down—wondering if we'd get there fast enough to have a chance at them. Our opportunity came on the edge of a field of dried-up sunflowers—the crop of seeds ready for harvesting, or the crane's crop. Wicker had us hunker down, but slinking discretely to our stations lining the field. We watched the birds first tiny and far away, calling and coming toward us. As they came closer we hugged the ground harder until, amazingly, they seemed just about overhead. Like the Canada geese Ed and I had pass-shot so many times before at home, the huge birds appeared to lumber along, looking larger and nearer than was reality; we knew to wait and that two shots per bird were needed. And when we'd each dispensed the second shell, two birds tumbled like collapsed umbrellas, out of the sky and crashing atop the sunflower stalks. Wicker Bill looked more than surprised, he looked downright dumbfounded.

As I watched Wicker collect the birds I admit I felt unsettled, something about the whole thing just didn't set right. I'd killed many birds, big and small, and happily anticipated the feast that a successful hunt guaranteed. Perhaps therein lay the rub: Every bird I'd shot previously I'd eaten and experienced the wonderful flavor prior to hunting it; I knew what glorious taste sensations lay in store. But this, this lawn ornament gone white and brown, how would this taste? I didn't have high hopes. And my distress was accentuated as I envisioned the challenge that lay before me in the kitchen. What appropriate cooking techniques might make these dinosaur doubles edible? How does one cook a sandhill crane?

Virtually every bird you can think of at some point in history has been eaten; and most considered quite a delicacy. The various species of crane are no exception. In the cooking encyclopedia and bible, *Larousse Gastronomique*, crane is described as "greatly prized" by the Romans who fattened it specially to give it a richer flavor. In the Middle ages, the crane was among the game birds eaten only in the best society. Queen Elizabeth's visit in the 16th century to Lord North included bringing 4,828 geese, capons, chickens, pigeons, quail, turkeys, swans, cranes and ducks, and 559 bitterns, shovelers, pewits, godwits, partridge, pheasant, to name but a partial list. From the Renaissance up to modern times, people ate albatross, cormorants, magpies, bustards, cranes, swans, storks, bitterns, falcons, egrets, sandpipers and many more. But as the entry on crane in *Larousse* further explains, "[crane is] seldom used as food nowadays…Only very young birds can be eaten." In other words the most encyclopedic and complete cookbook (with 8,500 recipes) of the 20th century had no recipe for crane. Plus determining the age of my two bathtub occupants seemed highly unlikely—damn, if only I'd had the presence of mind to ask how old they were before I pulled the trigger. The culinary methods of the Romans would provide no better clues for cooking crane: The Romans' favorite recipe for large birds required stuffing the cavity with asafetida—a disgustingly pungent herb known today, and with good reason, as "devil's dung." The only other treatment I could recall from history for preparing crane was recorded by 18th century epicurean Grimod de La Reynière who described this "Roast Without Equal" as: "an olive stuffed with capers and anchovies inside a figpecker inside an ortolan inside a lark inside a thrush inside a quail…" You get the picture, and of course it all ends up being inside a bustard or crane! I was in trouble.

But hey, I'd cooked all kinds of birds in the past, written detailed instructions, designed recipes and figured out what techniques were appropriate for which species. I could do this. Start with a review of the fundamental concepts for cooking birds, then peruse that mental index of bird recipes for a possible match to sandhill crane.

First, those basics:

- Consider every bird that comes into the kitchen on an individual basis but follow the general size rule that the smaller the bird the hotter and faster the cooking process.
- Then consider the individual bird's diet, overall condition, and care taken in the field dressing. All birds impart the flavor of what they've been feeding on and ingredients in a recipe can either accentuate and "tie" a taste, or mask it: complement the wild grape diet with a jelly sauce, stifle the fish-tinged meat by sautéing in milk.
- Wild birds are generally tougher. The theory being they're more athletic and have very little fat when compared to domesticated birds, so virtually all wild bird recipes must provide for additions of fat during cooking. Age, too, can be a factor in the toughness and/or dryness of the bird. Cooling the bird immediately after its demise helps tenderize the meat.
- Prolonged or multiple freezings will make a bird even tougher and drier.
- Removing the innards and blood quickly—both potential causes of a bitter or "gamy" flavor—guards against tainting of the meat.
- Try to leave the skin on. But skin on or off, add oil, bacon fat or butter during the cooking process to keep the bird from drying out. We all love a good fat—fortunately since game birds are low in fat and cholesterol we can afford to lather it on.
- All game birds are very high in protein and therefore continue cooking after being removed from the heat; this should be considered when testing for doneness, be sure to remove the bird from the oven before you think it is done. It is very easy to overcook game and again this will make it tough and lessen its innate good taste. Since game birds are high in protein they are very rich and a small portion can make a meal.

The basics were now considered, next came the mental perusal of the bird recipes I'd concocted over the years: Well, on that unpredictable October day in South Dakota the issue certainly wasn't how to cook an ostrich—for ostrich at least there are existing recipes and cooking techniques that follow form and logic. But the question was rather how to cook a sandhill crane, a bird with prehistoric peerage and a name that seemed to recall its cousin from the endangered species list. (No, Mother, that's a sandhill crane I've shot, not a whooping crane.) Indeed, our two sandhills' recent known history seemed to defy the very essence of proper game care and respect—no field dressing just a dump in the green bag, no refrigeration beyond the cold of the bathtub floor, and finally no plucking possible in the motel setting, just the eager-beaver knife of ol' Wicker Bill who would come—later—to "breast out" the birds. My assessment was that any attempt to apply the basics of correct game handling in the field had gone, basically, out the window of Wicker's truck somewhere between the frozen pothole and the rows of dead sunflower stalks.

The recipe route remained weak, too. Wicker was insistent that sandhill crane was delicious to eat but was vague about how to get it to the state of delectability. And I was struggling with the approach of using a recipe for a sister bird as template for crane: What, after all, was crane similar to? What lay now behind the shower curtain seemed more and more certainly to be the harbingers of a culinary disaster in the making. But the force of the hunter's mantra—to always eat what you've killed, to respectfully care for that which is to nourish—can drive even the most unadventurous and unenthusiastic of diners.

If you can't control the use of fundamental cooking concepts, or find a specific or adaptable recipe—try doing the next best thing: Throw caution to the wind and, with wild abandon (of course), wing it! One of the greatest attributes of cooking wild game is its surprises. It stretches the cook and the culinary adventure is really very exhilarating. Begin by remembering that one of the major causes for the implementation of the game laws and the elimination of the market hunter profession at the turn of this century was the gluttony and near extinction of many birds. Clearly, birds are innately great tasting. Next apply only the simplest and most straightforward methods for cooking; and choose to introduce other flavors that are familiar and of your own taste. Grilling my pterodactyl over an open fire, this cave man special, seemed only too fitting.

It was extraordinary. Tender, sweet, earthy dark meat, it conjured what Alexandre Dumas said of woodcock: "The meat of the woodcock is the only terrestrial food of the Gods." I beg to differ with Dumas, or at least to include sandhill crane as divine edible. But oh, I'd never have guessed by the look of the things.

Grilled Breast of Sandhill Crane
Green Beans and Beet Salad
Mascarpone Risotto
Chocolate Gelato

Serves four

GRILLED BREAST OF SANDHILL CRANE

- 1 sandhill crane, breasts removed
- ¼ cup olive oil
- 1 tsp. sea salt
- 1 tbsp. freshly ground pepper
- 2 tbsp. crushed juniper berries

Baste the breasts with olive oil, and season with sea salt, ground pepper. Pat the crushed juniper berries onto the breasts. Then grill the sandhill crane to a doneness of very rare, about 10 minutes total.

GREEN BEANS AND BEET SALAD

- 1 lb. green beans
- 8 medium-size beets
- 1 tbsp. vinegar
- 1 tsp. prepared mustard
- ½ cup olive or walnut oil
- Splash of soy sauce
- Salt and pepper
- Lettuce
- Mint

Blanch the beans in salted boiling water until they are just tender. Plunge them into ice water to stop the cooking and preserve the color. Drain them and let dry. Steam the beets until they are tender and can be pierced with a fork (about half an hour). Let them cool, peel and julienne them. Make a vinaigrette by combining in a blender the vinegar, mustard, oil, soy sauce, salt and pepper. Pour half the vinaigrette on the beets and half on the beans and toss each separately as the beets will bleed if you toss them too much together. Then toss the two vegetables together gently and serve on a bed of lettuce with a sprig of mint on each serving.

MASCARPONE RISOTTO

- 5 cups chicken stock
- 1 medium onion, chopped fine
- 2 tbsp. olive oil
- 1½ cups Arborio rice
- 4 tbsp. mascarpone
- ¼ cup grated parmesan cheese

Bring the chicken stock to a simmer in a pan on top of the stove. Let it remain simmering and meanwhile in a large fry pan sauté the onion in the olive oil until it is translucent. Add the rice and cook for five minutes, stirring. Add 2 cups of the hot chicken stock and cook slowly, adding more stock a little at a time as it is absorbed by the rice. Once you have added all the stock and it is almost completely absorbed, add the mascarpone and parmesan cheese and cook for 1 minute more and serve.

CHOCOLATE GELATO

- 3 cups whole milk
- 1 cup sugar
- 3 tbsp. cornstarch
- ¾ cup unsweetened cocoa
  (Enough ice and salt for processing in your ice cream maker)

Bring 2 cups of the milk to a simmer in a medium-size pan and then remove from the heat. In a small saucepan add the remaining cup of milk, the sugar, cornstarch, and cocoa and cook until the sugar and cocoa have dissolved, stirring well. Add this milk mixture to the hot milk and cook, stirring, until it has thickened slightly, about 8 to 10 minutes. Let it cool and then pour into a bowl and cover with plastic wrap and place in the fridge overnight. Process the gelato the next day in the ice cream maker per the manufacturer's instructions.

Quail for the Campfire
Grilled Red Onion
Charcoal Grilled Bread
Almond Cake

Serves four

This menu is designed for you to use the first night of an ooh la la camping trip. You can have each item completely prepped and ready to go on the campfire. But, of course, they can be cooked right at home either in an oven or on your outdoor grill.

Good, extra virgin olive oil is important to many of the recipes in this book, but particularly to this bread. I recommend ordering some from a catalog if you can't get a great oil locally.

QUAIL FOR THE CAMPFIRE

    Salt and pepper
4 quail
    Fresh rosemary and thyme leaves or 1 tbsp. each dried rosemary and thyme per bird
4 bacon strips

Salt and pepper the cavity of each bird and stuff with the fresh herbs. Truss and wrap first with a strip of bacon and then with buttered parchment paper and foil (several layers of parchment paper—two of the foil). Place in hot cinders for 35 minutes. Be sure to turn the birds every so often and renew the foil/paper if necessary.

GRILLED RED ONION

2 red onions
2 tbsp. unsalted butter or good green oil
    Salt and pepper

Slice the onions ¼-inch thick and grill them lightly for 2-3 minutes per side either over the campfire or in the broiler. Now sauté the grilled onion slices quickly in the butter over a medium heat or dribble with a good olive oil for a more salad-like taste. Season with salt and pepper.

CHARCOAL GRILLED BREAD

1 loaf of French bread
1 garlic clove, halved
½ cup good green olive oil

Slice the bread into ½-inch pieces and rub each side with the garlic. Grill over a medium-low fire and then pour a little of the olive oil on each piece.

ALMOND CAKE

¾ cup almonds
6 tbsp. unsalted butter
⅔ cup sugar
3 eggs
½ cup sifted all-purpose flour
3 tbsp. brandy
   Dusting of confectioners' sugar

Roast the almonds on a cookie sheet in a 300° oven for about 20 minutes or until they are a nice golden tan. Be sure to shake the almonds often while cooking so they do not get over-done. Chop the almonds very fine. This can be done in a food processor if you like.

Melt the butter and when cooled stir in the sugar and eggs. Then add the flour, almonds and brandy.

Butter and flour an 8-inch square pan and pour the batter into it. Bake at 325° for 20 minutes or until a skewer pulls out clean when you stick it in the center of the cake. Let cool in the pan, then cut into squares and dust with the confectioners' sugar.

Green Grape Quail
Wild Rice with Walnuts
Sliced Tomatoes with Fresh Basil
Crème Brulée

Serves four

This menu you might think about using early on in the quail season when the fresh basil and tomatoes are still easily obtainable from a garden or vegetable stand. Nothing is worse in my mind than having to serve those pale orange, hard balls packaged in plastic baskets and cellophane. Don't be scared off by the use of grape leaves in the quail recipe. They are very often found in chain supermarkets or if you are fortunate to live in a rural area, you can pick them fresh from the wild—wash them carefully. Of course, you can substitute by using foil, although this is, obviously, not as much fun.

The cooking method for the wild rice—that of covering the rice with 3 inches of water and boiling it all without a lid until the water has evaporated—is one that I discovered from an enclosure in a package of the wild grain and works with any amount of wild rice. It also is a method which insures doneness and doesn't involve all that ridiculous soaking which is so often recommended.

The crème brulée suggested here is a more liquid one than is sometimes served. If you like your crème brulée to resemble the consistency of week-old refrigerated Jell-O you will need to cook this recipe at least twice as long.

GREEN GRAPE QUAIL

  Salt and pepper
4 quail
4 strips of bacon
8 grape leaves
  Butter
1 lb. seedless green grapes

Salt and pepper each quail and wrap first in bacon and then in 2 grape leaves. Use butcher's twine to hold the bacon and grape leaves in place. Put wrapped quail in a buttered pan and cut a piece of parchment paper to fit over the top of the birds. Butter the side of the paper which touches the birds. Cover birds and paper and a lid and cook at 425° for 15 minutes. Add the grapes and baste the birds with the juices. Cook for 10 minutes more.

WILD RICE WITH WALNUTS

½ cup wild rice
⅓ cup walnuts, chopped
1 tbsp. unsalted butter
  Salt and pepper

Cook the rice by putting it in a sauce pan with enough water so it is covered by 3 inches. Bring it to a boil and then simmer it uncovered until all the water has evaporated, about ½ to ¾ of an hour. Toast the chopped walnuts while you cook the wild rice. When the rice is done add the butter, salt, and pepper. Toss in the toasted walnuts and serve.

CRÈME BRULÉE

    6 eggs
    5 tbsp. sugar
    3 cups heavy cream (or 1½ cups heavy cream and 1½ cups whipping cream)
    1 tbsp. vanilla
½ to ⅔ cup dark brown sugar

Separate the eggs, beat the yolks and combine well with the white sugar and cream. Heat the mixture over a medium heat stirring constantly with a whisk until you can see steam beginning to rise and the custard is starting to form around the edge of the pot. Remove from the burner and add the vanilla. Pour through a strainer into a round, stoneware baking dish that is about 11 inches or so in diameter. Put the dish on a cookie sheet that has sides and surround it with an inch or so of boiling water. Bake it in a preheated oven at 300° for 30 minutes or until the custard is just setting around the edges but is still soft in the middle. Remove from the oven and let it sit in the water-bath while it cools—about 30 minutes. Then refrigerate the custard for at least two hours or overnight. Just before serving sprinkle the custard with the brown sugar and put the dish back on the cookie sheet and this time surround it with ice cubes. Put it under a very hot broiler for a minute or two until the brown sugar burns a bit and forms a nice hard crust. Serve immediately or chill again and serve.

Grouse Pancetta
Julienned Celery and Zucchini
Fried Polenta
Poached Prunes and Apricots with Cognac and Cream

Serves four

If you are unfamiliar with pancetta I recommend it most highly. It is essentially Italian-cured bacon and ranges in quality depending where you buy it. It can be bought in almost any supermarket delicatessen or Italian market.

Polenta is a starch and an excellent alternative to the ones you get so tired of serving. A form of polenta was used as a staple by the Roman soldiers when they fought against Hannibal, which says nothing about its taste but does date its use. Listed in almost all the general cookbooks (*Joy of Cooking*, *New York Times Cookbook*) I find it interesting that it is so rarely served. So try it, you will like it.

GROUSE PANCETTA

- 1 lb. pancetta slices
- 1 garlic clove, peeled
- 1 cup fresh sage leaves, plus 12 leaves for atop the birds
- Salt and pepper
- 4 whole grouse, either plucked or skinned
- Oil

Dice about half the pancetta slices into ⅛-inch pieces. Crush the garlic and add it to the pancetta along with a few sage leaves and salt and pepper to taste. Stuff each bird with the mixture and truss. Place several sage leaves and then whole slices of pancetta on each bird and wrap in parchment paper bag painted with oil. Roast at 350° for 40 minutes. Open it up at the table, the aroma is splendid!

JULIENNED CELERY AND ZUCCHINI

- 6 stalks celery
- 1 zucchini
- 2 tbsp. unsalted butter
- Salt and pepper

Scrape the outside of each celery stalk (except for the young tender ones) with a vegetable peeler and cut into 2-inch lengths. Now julienne into ⅛-inch sticks. Cut the zucchini skin off in thick strips, discard the interior part of the zucchini and then julienne the skin into ⅛-inch sticks. Sauté the celery and zucchini together in butter till they are hot but still crisp. Season with salt and pepper.

FRIED POLENTA

- 1 onion
- ½ cup (1 stick) unsalted butter
- 3 cups milk
- 1 cup cornmeal
- 1 cup water
- ½ tsp. nutmeg
- Salt and pepper
- Fat to fry in (from bacon or pancetta or use butter)

Chop the onion very fine and sauté it in the butter till translucent. Add the milk and bring it to a boil. Combine the cornmeal and water, stir with a fork, and then add it to the boiling milk and onion mixture. Stir continuously until the mixture is so thick the spoon stands up in it. Remove it from the heat and add the nutmeg and season with salt and pepper. Grease a cookie sheet and spread the polenta ½-inch to ¼-inch thick on it. Let stand until cool and slightly hardened. Now cut with cookie cutters and fry the shapes in the fat till they are brown. Serve.

POACHED PRUNES AND APRICOTS WITH COGNAC AND CREAM

- 12 orange rind slivers
- 12 lemon rind slivers
- 1 bottle of good white wine
- Several whole cloves
- ½ lb. pitted and dried prunes
- ½ lb. dried apricots
- 1 cup cream
- ⅛ cup cognac or Armagnac

Shave an orange and a lemon with a potato peeler making sure not to get any white part of the rind. Put 12 of the shavings from the orange and 12 from the lemon into a pan with the wine and cloves. Bring the mixture to a boil and let simmer for a few minutes. Add the prunes and apricots and let sit for 48 hours or more.

When ready to serve, whip the cream with the cognac in it and serve on top of the fruit.

Spitted Woodcock
Green Beans with Wild Mushrooms
Baked Goat Cheese
Meyer Lemon Sherbet

Serves four

The grape leaves are found in most supermarkets or can also be gathered in the wild. You also can leave them out of this recipe entirely if you can't find any.

Don't feel that you must instantly become a wild mushroom expert and run into the woods with your basket in order to follow this menu. True wild mushroom experts are hard to come by and, as in our case, are knowledgeable about only a very small number of wild mushroom varieties. But most of us who eat wild mushrooms seem to have two methods of obtaining them: Learn one or possibly two types of absolutely distinct, non-harmful mushrooms, like chanterelles or chicken-of-the-woods, and never pick anything else. Or, buy them dried which you can do more and more easily as people tire of the blander tasting cultivated mushrooms.

SPITTED WOODCOCK

- 8 whole woodcock, skinned
- 8 bacon strips
- 8 grape leaves
- French bread slices (10 or so depending on the way the birds are spitted)
- 4 oz. unsalted butter (½ stick) at room temperature and cut into bits, plus enough for buttering the bread slices
- 4 tbsp. Armagnac or cognac
- 1⅓ cups stock
- Salt and pepper

Truss each bird and wrap first in a strip of bacon and then in a grape leaf. Spit the birds placing a buttered piece of French bread on either side of each bird. Lay the skewered birds and bread in a roasting pan and cook in the oven at 450° for 20 minutes. After cooking, place the birds and bread on heated plates. In the roasting pan add the cognac. Scraping the bottom of the pan with a wire whisk add the stock and, over a high flame, cook until the liquid is reduced to about ¾ cup. Now whisk in the butter and season with salt and pepper. This is meant to be just a moistener for the birds, not a real sauce.

GREEN BEANS WITH WILD MUSHROOMS

    1 lb. green beans
    1 oz. dried wild mushrooms
    2 tbsp. unsalted butter
      Salt and pepper

Blanch the green beans and then chill them immediately in ice water. Reconstitute the mushrooms in a little warm water (if dried). Rinse the mushrooms in cool water saving the reconstituted juice. Reduce the juice in a sauté pan (be sure not to get any of the mushrooms' grit in the pan) until it is just a glaze on the bottom of the pan. Melt the butter with the glaze and add the mushrooms and beans. Sauté quickly, then season with salt and pepper.

BAKED GOAT CHEESE

    4 ½-inch slices of goat cheese (or an amount that looks appropriate for four individual servings)
    ½ cup olive oil
      Sprig of fresh thyme
    1 tsp. dried thyme
    ⅔ cup fine-sifted bread crumbs
      Lettuce leaves (Bibb or Boston mixed with bittergreens are good) tossed with a tasty vinaigrette

Marinate the slices of cheese in the olive oil and thyme sprig for a day or more.

Mix the dried thyme with bread crumbs and dredge the slices of marinated cheese in the dry mixture making sure to cover the slices well. Bake in a preheated oven at 400° for about 5 minutes till the cheese just starts to bubble. Place the lettuce on individual salad plates and, with a spatula, lay the cheese on top. Serve immediately.

MEYER LEMON SHERBET

- 7-8 Meyer lemons (to make 1 cup of juice)
- 1½ cups sugar
- 1½ cups water
- 1 tbsp. at least Meyer lemon rind, slivered and chopped fine
- ¾ cup whole milk
- 2 tbsp. water
- 1 tsp. gelatin
- (Enough kosher salt and ice cubes for your ice cream machine)

Juice the Meyer lemons, making sure you have a full cup, and reserve the rind from one of the lemons. In a small saucepan combine the sugar and water and heat until the sugar is completely dissolved. Sliver the lemon rind and chop fine. In a bowl, pour the sugar water and the lemon juice and add in the milk and lemon rind. In the saucepan put the 2 tablespoons of water and stir in the gelatin and let it sit until the gelatin has plumped up-about a minute or two. Then heat it gently so there is no graininess. Stir in the gelatin now to the lemon-milk mixture, cover the bowl with plastic wrap, and refrigerate for at least six hours until it is very cold. Then freeze it according to the instructions with your ice cream maker.

Dove Salad
Cornsticks
Tangerine Sorbet

Serves four

I know, I know. It is a terrible pain in the neck to pluck and roast these little tiny birdies, particularly as you throw out the skin later. It is okay to use skinned birds but roasting dove in the skin is better. And remember, there has been some trouble and expense gone to getting them in the first place.

Walnut oil is expensive and does go rancid more readily than most cooking oils, so you might consider splitting a bottle with a friend. It is a great addition to this and many recipes and worth ordering if not available locally.

Sorbets and ices, I have found, are very dependent on the liqueur that is added and I think it wise, particularly with this sorbet, to try and use the Mandarin Napoleon recommended. It truly adds to the flavor.

DOVE SALAD

- 6 roasted dove
- 6 bacon strips
- 1 cup white wine
- 1 tbsp. vinegar
- ⅛ tsp. salt
- Ground pepper
- ¼ tsp. prepared mustard
- ¼ cup walnut oil
- 1 head chicory or escarole
- 1 head Bibb lettuce
- ½ cup walnuts
- 2 tbsp. unsalted butter

Wrap the dove in bacon strips, truss, and place in a small roasting pan. Pour white wine into the pan and cook in a pre-heated oven at 400° for 20 minutes. Let cool and then remove the meat from the bones. Discard the skin and chop the meat into small pieces. Now in the roasting pan where the dove cooked combine the vinegar, salt, a few pepper grinds, the mustard and the walnut oil. Whisk this together over a low flame.

Wash the chicory and Bibb lettuce. Sauté the walnuts in butter and chop. Now toss the dove, lettuce and walnuts together in a bowl with the vinegar mixture. Add salt and pepper or lemon juice to taste.

CORNSTICKS

- 1½ cups cornmeal
- 2 tsp. baking powder
- 1 tsp. salt
- ¼ cup flour
- 2 tbsp. sugar
- 2 eggs
- 1 cup buttermilk
- 3 tbsp. bacon drippings

Sift together the cornmeal, baking powder, salt, flour and sugar. Beat the eggs, then add the buttermilk and bacon drippings and combine with the dry ingredients. Pour batter into buttered muffin tins or cornstick molds. Bake in a 425° oven for 15 minutes (molds) or 25 minutes (tins).

TANGERINE SORBET

- 15-20 tangerines (enough for 4 cups)
- 1 cup sugar
- Pinch of salt
- Splash of lemon juice
- 1 tbsp. Mandarin Napoleon liqueur (tangerine liqueur)
- (Remember to have enough ice and salt for your ice cream freezer, too).

Squeeze enough tangerines so you have 1 quart of juice. Boil ½ cup of water and add the sugar and cook for 5 minutes. Let cool. Add the sugar syrup to the fruit juice as needed to please your taste. Add the salt and lemon juice to help the taste and then pour in the liqueur. Chill the mixture in the canister from your ice cream maker. Then freeze according to the ice cream machine's directions.

Fried Dove
Zucchini Fans with Tomatoes
Gorgonzola Polenta
Toll House Cookies

Serves four

In a cookbook I once read, polenta was described as "hardtack," perhaps because plain polenta, like most starches, has a blandness similar to the hard biscuits once used by soldiers. Polenta's taste depends strongly on how it is cooked and what can be added to it. This, of course, is one of the great virtues of any starch; particularly so with polenta. Cheese is a great addition to polenta.

Toll House cookies seem a little silly to put in a menu cookbook. But clearly they are a most favorite cookie and should be baked more often. Use the recipe on the back of the Nestle Chocolate Chip package. And, in this one exception to my rule of always using unsalted butter, I think chocolate chip cookies come out better using salted butter.

FRIED DOVE

- ½ cup flour
- ¼ tsp. dried thyme
- Salt and pepper
- 2 eggs
- 2 tsp. oil
- 2 tsp. water
- 10 dove, breasted out
- 1½ cups fine bread crumbs (strained)
- ½ cup (1 stick) clarified unsalted butter

Combine the flour, thyme and a dash of salt and pepper. Combine the eggs, oil and water and mix well. Dip the breasts first in the flour mixture, then in the egg mixture and finally in the crumbs, making sure to thoroughly coat the breasts with each dip. Let the breasts rest on a cake rack for 20 minutes or so. Heat enough clarified butter over a medium flame to cover the pan bottom by ⅛ inch. Cook the breasts 1 to 2 minutes per side till they are lightly brown and done to the touch.

ZUCCHINI FANS WITH TOMATOES

- 6 small zucchini
- 4 small tomatoes
- Fresh basil
- 3 tbsp. unsalted butter
- Salt and pepper

Make four deep cuts from top to bottom into each zucchini, slicing almost to the base and creating a fan out of each zucchini. Slice the tomatoes and slip them into the zucchini cuts. Arrange carefully in a buttered baking dish and sprinkle with basil. Dot with butter and bake in a 350° oven for 20 minutes or until tender. Place in a serving dish with a spatula and season with salt and pepper.

GORGONZOLA POLENTA

- 1 small onion chopped fine (optional)
- 2 cups milk
- 6 tbsp. unsalted butter
- ¾ cup cornmeal
- 5 oz. gorgonzola, diced
- ½ tsp. nutmeg
- 1 tsp. kosher salt
- ½ cup heavy cream
- Pepper to taste

If you are using the onion, sauté it in the butter until translucent.

Then, in a small saucepan, bring the onion, milk, and butter to a boil. Add the cornmeal slowly, stirring constantly till thick and the spoon can stand up in it. Be careful as the polenta will spit at you. Remove from the heat and add the cheese, nutmeg, salt, cream and pepper and mix well. Turn immediately into buttered muffin tins and let rest till set. Remove from the tin and put in a heavy oven-proof pan and cook at 400° for 15 minutes (if you like, you can add a little more cheese to the tops of the polenta muffins before putting them in the oven.)

Preserved Woodcock with Olives
Basil Pasta
Sun-dried Tomato Bread
Cantaloupe Ice

Serves four

The concept of cooking and eating an undrawn bird comes from Europe where it is quite common and anyone who has spent time there can't understand having a game cookbook without recipes for birds in the round. This, however, does not mean you have to try it. I have not, although Ed has and says it is quite good.

Sun-dried tomatoes, listed in the next recipe, are no longer very difficult to find. Most often found in gourmet shops or most good grocery stores, just like any other dried fruit. They also are available packed in oil at a higher cost. They are wonderful and worth keeping on hand to dress up a salad, a bread, or a pasta.

The cantaloupe ice is very dependent on using a ripe, maybe even an over-ripe cantaloupe. It is not worth the trouble without one and raspberry or peach should be substituted.

PRESERVED WOODCOCK WITH OLIVES

- 4 woodcock
- 8 oz. black, pitted Nicoise olives
- 8 oz. salt pork, cut into sticks 1 inch by ¼ inch
- 1 qt. water
- Salt and pepper
- 4 garlic cloves, peeled and crushed
- 2 large sprigs (or 3 tsp. dried) of thyme
- ½ tsp. rosemary
- 20 peppercorns
- 8 juniper berries
- 5 tbsp. olive oil
- 3 tbsp. cognac

Pluck the woodcock and leave them in the round (undrawn).

In a saucepan put the olives, salt pork and 1 quart water. Bring the water to a boil and then simmer for 5 minutes. Drain in a strainer and then rinse the olives in cold water.

In a tureen arrange the woodcock and sprinkle them with salt and pepper, the crushed garlic, thyme, rosemary, peppercorns, juniper berries, and the olive/salt pork combination. Combine the olive oil, cognac and a little water and paint each bird with it. Cover the tureen with a tight-fitting lid and cook in a preheated oven at 250° for 4 hours. The meat should be so soft it could be spread.

BASIL PASTA

- 1 cup olive oil
- 2 large cloves garlic
- 1 bay leaf
- ⅓ cup vinegar
- Touch of lemon juice
- 1 tbsp. prepared mustard
- Salt and pepper
- 1 large bunch fresh basil
- 1 lb. pasta
- Hot pepper flakes
- 6 oz. goat cheese, crumbled

In the cup of olive oil cook the peeled garlic cloves over a medium-low heat for about 20 minutes or until the garlic is soft but still holds its shape. Add the bay leaf while it is still hot and let sit overnight.

Make a little vinaigrette with the vinegar, lemon juice, mustard and salt and pepper. Pour the vinaigrette into a blender and add the basil with the stems removed and the olive oil garlic (less the bay leaf). Blend till smooth. Check for seasoning.

Cook the pasta particularly al dente (it will absorb the moisture from the basil mixture and become mushy if cooked till soft). Drain the pasta, cool a little (or it will discolor the basil vinaigrette and make its brilliant green appearance not so attractive) and toss with the basil vinaigrette. Sprinkle with red pepper flakes and crumbled goat cheese. Decorate with any extra little basil leaves.

SUN-DRIED TOMATO BREAD

- 2 cups lukewarm to warm water
- 1 tbsp. dry yeast
- 1 tbsp. sugar
- 1 tbsp. salt
- 5 cups all-purpose flour
- ½ cup sun-dried tomatoes
- ¼ cup olive oil
- Sprig of thyme
- ¼ cup wine
- ⅓ cup pitted black olives, chopped coarsely
- Butter or oil for greasing pans

In the bowl of a standing mix master, fitted with a bread hook, add the warm water and sprinkle in the yeast, sugar, and salt. Let sit for a few minutes until the yeast looks dissolved and foamy. Now pour in 5 cups of flour and mix at the lowest setting, usually marked "stir," until the flour is blended and then increase the speed to the next level, #2. Continue blending at this speed until the dough is well mixed, pulling away from the sides of the bowl, and forming a ball. Reconstitute the tomatoes by cooking them in the oil, thyme, and wine over a medium-low heat until they are soft. Let them cool and then chop them coarsely. Add both the olive and the reconstituted tomatoes to the dough. Turn onto a floured surface and knead the dough for about 8 minutes. It should be slightly tacky to the touch but smooth and very malleable. Place in a bowl that has been oiled, turn the dough over in the oil so the top is oiled, too, and cover the bowl with a cloth. Let rise until it is double in size, about 2 to 3 hours. Punch it down and let it rest while you prepare the pan(s) for it to rise in again.

This recipe makes enough for a baguette and a loaf. I always make a baguette for the week's spaghetti night so I pull a handful of dough off and roll it into a big snake and lay it in one side of a baguette pan that has been buttered. The remaining dough I use to make the Sun-dried Tomato bread for this menu by forming a ball with the dough, flouring it heavily, and putting it into a banneton, also heavily floured. Both the baguette and the round I cover with a cloth and let rise again for another hour or so.

Using a banneton can be a bit tricky but it produces a beautiful round of bread. Using a piece of parchment paper, floured, atop the back of a cookie sheet, I carefully invert the banneton and let the dough fall out.

Often it loses its rise and I let it sit covered for another hour to rise again. Once the round is ready to bake I slide it onto a pizza stone that is in a preheated oven at 420° and bake it and the baguette for 35 to 40 minutes or until golden. Once baked, I turn the baguette out onto a cooling rack and slide the round on the parchment onto the cookie sheet—also onto the rack to cool. Let cool for 30 minutes or so before cutting.

If I don't plan to use the baguette that day I wrap it in foil and put it in the freezer to use another day. (It just needs to be taken from the freezer and put in a preheated oven at 350° for 30 minutes or so.) .

CANTALOUPE ICE

- 2 very ripe cantaloupes
- ¾ cup confectioners' sugar
- A pinch of salt
- Lemon juice to taste
- 1 tbsp. white rum

(Make sure you have enough ice and salt for your ice cream machine)

Halve the cantaloupes and scoop out the seeds. Now scoop out the fruit and make sure you have about 1 quart. Purée the cantaloupe in a blender and then add the sugar, salt, and lemon juice sparingly until the mixture tastes right. Now add the rum and make any adjustments for taste. Place the cantaloupe mixture in the canister of your ice cream machine and place in the refrigerator for a couple of hours. Then freeze it in the machine according to the manufacturer's directions. For a nice effect you can pack the ice cream back into the cantaloupe shells.

Juniper Encrusted Woodcock in Rosemary Cream Sauce
Leg of Lamb
White Bean Purée
Green Salad
Stuffed Oranges

Serves four

This woodcock hors d'oeuvre became one of my signature game recipes during my years of hunting woodcock in New Brunswick, Canada. The Peterborough, New Hampshire boys loved it. So when I was an expert editor of the 75th anniversary edition of the *Joy of Cooking*, I included it in the game section.

We've recommended soaking the white beans for only an hour. That overnight business is passé and a leftover from the trading post days.

If you don't have a favorite way to cook a leg of lamb, here is a method I recommend:

Remove all the fat from a 6-8 pound leg of lamb. Stick slivers of garlic and leaves of rosemary randomly into it at an angle and brush with olive oil. Let sit in the refrigerator for 1-2 days. Cook in a preheated oven at 400° for 12 minutes per pound.

JUNIPER ENCRUSTED WOODCOCK IN ROSEMARY CREAM SAUCE

- 4 woodcock (or dove or squab)
- 2 tbsp. juniper berries, chopped
- 2 tbsp. olive oil
- 3 tbsp. Armagnac
- ½ cup heavy cream
- 1 tbsp. fresh rosemary, chopped
-   Salt, pepper

Breast out the woodcock and slice each breast into strips and roll in the chopped juniper berries. Sauté the woodcock strips in hot oil very fast (about 30 seconds, the meat should still be pink) and then remove them from the pan and place on a warm platter. Add the Armagnac to the juices left in the pan and stir with a wire whisk making sure to scrape the bottom. Now add the cream and cook on a high heat till thick and reduced to about half the original quantity. Whisk in the rosemary. Season the cooked woodcock with salt and pepper and pour the sauce over the meat. Serve with toothpicks for an hors d'oeuvre or over homemade angel-hair pasta for supper.

WHITE BEAN PURÉE

- 1 lb. white beans, soaked an hour
- 2½ cups chicken stock
- 2½ cups water
- 1 onion
- 2 whole cloves
- 1 bay leaf
- Pinch of thyme
- A few parsley stems
- Salt and pepper
- ¾ cup heavy cream
- ½ cup (1 stick) unsalted butter, softened

Drain the soaking beans and pour in the broth and water (if you don't have any chicken stock, all water and 2 chicken bouillon cubes is fine). Peel the onion and push the cloves into it. Add the onion, bay leaf, thyme, parsley stems and salt and pepper to the bean pot and bring to a boil. Simmer until the beans are tender (about ½ to 1 hour). Remove bay leaf. In small batches, churn up the bean mixture in a food processor, zipping it for 1 second so as not to purée but just to break-up the skins of the beans. Push through a strainer back into the pot and mix in the cream and butter. Reheat gently and season with salt and pepper.

STUFFED ORANGES

- 4 large navel oranges
- 1 qt. orange ice or sherbet
- Sprigs of mint

Cut off the top of each orange and pith and scoop out the orange inside. Rinse and let drain. Soften the sherbet or ice and then fill each orange shell. Refreeze and then decorate with sprigs of mint.

Quail Soup
Pasta with Chestnuts and Pignolis
Olive Oil and Salt Bread
Custard Oranges

Serves four

The olive oil and salt bread will be a flop if you don't use a good green olive oil and the kosher salt. Also, making the ¼-inch holes is difficult and the utmost care should be taken. It is terrific bread and worth the trouble.

Whenever you make a custard dessert—actually any dessert that is egg based—flavoring (as in this case the Cointreau) is essential. If the liqueur cabinet cannot provide it, vanilla is a good substitute.

QUAIL SOUP

- 10 quail, skinned
- 4 tbsp. unsalted butter
- 1 large carrot, chopped fine
- 2 shallots or onions, chopped fine
- 1½ qts. chicken stock
- Bouquet garni
- 2-3 juniper berries
- 4 tbsp. rice
- 4 slices French bread cut into ½-inch cubes
- 2 tbsp. olive oil
- 2 cups cream
- Salt and pepper
- 3 tbsp. sour cream

Remove the breasts from the quail and set aside. Crush and break up the remaining carcasses and brown them in half of the butter in a stockpot or Dutch oven. Add the carrot and shallots, toss, then cover the pan and cook over a low flame for 15 minutes. Add the stock and bring to a boil. Add the bouquet garni, juniper berries and rice. Reduce the heat to very low and simmer for 2 hours.

Cube the French bread and fry in the olive oil. Set aside.

Slice the quail breasts on the diagonal and sauté quickly (about 30 seconds) in the remaining butter. Set aside.

Bring cream to a boil and reduce to simmer. Stir every now and then until it is halved in quantity and thickens. Set aside.

Once the carcasses have simmered for two hours remove from the pot and let cool. Pick any meat or skin off the bones and along with the vegetables, grind in a food processor or blender. Push the puree through a strainer, scraping the bottom, and then return it to the broth. Bring it to a boil and stir in the reduced cream and pieces of breast meat, reduce heat and let simmer for 5 minutes. Check taste for salt and pepper. Remove from the heat and blend in the sour cream. Add the croutons just before serving.

PASTA WITH CHESTNUTS AND PIGNOLIS

½ lb. chestnuts
¼ cup pignolis
4 tbsp. unsalted butter
1 cup heavy cream
1 tsp. dried sage leaves
½ lb. prepared pasta
Salt and pepper

Make a deep "X" on the tip of each of the chestnuts and then roast under the broiler till their shells are slightly black and cracked. Let them cool then peel and slice them so you have about ¼ cup of chestnuts. Sauté the pignolis in half of the butter till light brown then add the remaining butter and chestnuts and sauté a bit more. Reduce the cream by letting it boil slowly in a frying pan till it is halved in quantity then add the sage. Cook the pasta, drain and wash, and return it to the cooking pan and toss with the cream. Add the pignolis and chestnuts and check for seasoning.

OLIVE OIL AND SALT BREAD

- 2 cups lukewarm to warm water
- 1 tbsp. dry yeast
- 1 tbsp. sugar
- 1 tbsp. salt
- 2 tbsp. dried thyme
- 5 cups or so of all-purpose flour (I recommend King Arthur Flour)
- ¼ cup good green olive oil
- 1 tbsp. kosher salt
- Butter and oil for greasing pans

In the bowl of a standing mix master, fitted with a bread hook, add the warm water and sprinkle in the yeast, sugar, salt, and thyme. Let sit for a few minutes until the yeast looks dissolved and foamy. Now pour in 5 cups of flour and mix at the lowest setting, usually marked "stir," until the flour is blended and then increase the speed to the next level, #2. Continue blending at this speed until the dough is well mixed, pulling away from the sides of the bowl, and forming a ball. Turn onto a floured surface and knead the dough for about 8 minutes. It should be slightly tacky to the touch but smooth and very malleable. Place in a bowl that has been oiled, turn the dough over in the oil so the top is oiled, too, and cover the bowl with a cloth. Let rise until it is double in size, about 2 to 3 hours. Punch it down and let it rest while you prepare the pan(s) for it to rise in again.

This recipe makes enough for a baguette and a loaf. I always make a baguette for the week's spaghetti night so I pull a handful of dough off and roll it into a big snake and lay it in one side of a baguette pan that has been buttered. The remaining dough I use to make the Olive Oil and Salt Bread for this menu by forming a ball with the dough, flouring it heavily, and putting it into a banneton, also heavily floured. Both the baguette and the round I cover with a cloth and let rise again for another hour or so.

Using a banneton can be a bit tricky but it produces a beautiful round of bread. Using a piece of parchment paper, floured, atop the back of a cookie sheet, I carefully invert the banneton and let the dough fall out. I then very carefully poke ¼-inch holes all around the top of the bread with the end of a wooden spoon. Fill the holes with the olive oil (or you can use walnut oil) and sprinkle with the kosher salt Often it loses its rise and I let it sit covered for another hour to rise again. Once the round is ready to bake I slide it onto a pizza stone that is in a preheated oven at 420º and bake it and the baguette for 35 to 40 minutes or until golden. Once baked, I turn the baguette out onto a cooling rack and slide the round on the parchment onto the cookie sheet—also onto the rack to cool. Let cool for 30 minutes or so before cutting.

If I don't plan to use the baguette that day I wrap it in foil and put it in the freezer to use another day. (It just needs to be taken from the freezer and put in a preheated oven at 350º for 30 minutes or so.) .

CUSTARD ORANGES

    4 large navel oranges
    3 egg yolks
    ⅓ cup sugar
    1½ oz. Cointreau
    1⅓ cups heavy cream
        Cocoa powder

Cut off the top of each orange and scoop out the inside. Rinse and let drain. Beat the egg yolks and sugar together then add the Cointreau. Now whip one cup of the cream until it is stiff. Mix in ⅓ of the whipped cream and then fold in the remaining cream. Fill each orange with the egg-cream mixture and set on a plate in the refrigerator for at least two hours. When ready to serve whip the remaining ⅓ cup cream and put a dollop on each orange top. Dust with cocoa.

Pheasant Sandwich
Ruffed Grouse Sandwich with Hazelnut Butter
Cold Wild Rice Salad
Assorted Cheeses (Brie, Goat, Saga)
Olives
Fresh Fruit
Cookies and Cheese

Serves four

Ruffed grouse have always been one of my favorite upland birds to eat. Unfortunately, they are also very difficult for me to shoot; making them into sandwich meat is almost more than I can bear. Fortunately, I've had the pleasure of hunting with many a good grouse hunters. In the early days it was Richard Montague. Mr. Montague not only made his own beer, spoke several dead languages, owned a series of well-mannered Brittanys and a pretty little bicycle shop in remote Strafford, Vermont, but he managed to fill his freezer with 30 to 40 grouse each season. It is to characters such as Richard that this recipe is dedicated.

For some reason upland birds are more difficult to pluck than water fowl. The skin tears more readily and, particularly in the case of pheasant, the feathers are more difficult to pull out. Consequently, I suggest using this recipe on leftover pheasant so you get two meals for the work of one plucking. Another alternative to plucking for sandwich meat is to save this recipe for the times the hunter visits his happy pheasant preserve. Most private pheasant preserve owners ask their hunters if they would prefer to take home the specific birds shot that day or ones already plucked and cleaned. Certainly for a sandwich-meat bird, pride of ownership can be foregone.

PHEASANT SANDWICH

- 1 cup (2 sticks) unsalted butter
- ½ tbsp. basil
- 1 finely chopped shallot
- ¼ tsp. grated lemon rind
- Slices of French bread (enough to accommodate the amount of pheasant you have)
- Leftover pheasant or roast pheasant sliced thin
- Watercress
- Salt and pepper

Whip the butter until it is fluffy. Reconstitute the basil in a little hot water and add it to the butter along with the shallot and lemon rind. Spread French bread thickly with the compound butter and lay on the pheasant and watercress. Season with salt and pepper.

RUFFED GROUSE SANDWICH WITH HAZELNUT BUTTER

- ½ cup hazelnuts
- 1 cup (2 sticks) unsalted butter
- 1 tbsp. finely chopped parsley
- Salt and pepper
- Slices of whole wheat bread
- 2 grouse, roasted and cooled and sliced thin

Toast the hazelnuts on a cookie sheet in the oven till they are brown. Be careful not to burn them. Remove the nuts from the oven and cover with a tea towel for 15 minutes or so to create steam, then rub off the skins with the tea towel. Chop finely. Whip the butter and add the nuts, chopped parsley, salt and pepper to taste. Spread whole wheat bread thickly with the compound butter and lay thin slices of grouse on top.

COLD WILD RICE SALAD

½ cup wild rice
4-5 radishes
1 cup green seedless grapes
2 tbsp. vinegar
½ cup olive oil
1 tsp. prepared mustard
1 shallot, chopped
1 tsp. tarragon

Place the rice in a pot with 3 inches of water covering it. Bring to a boil and then turn the heat down and let simmer, uncovered, until all the water is gone (about 30 minutes). Slice the radishes very thin. Cut the grapes in half. Toss the radishes and grapes in with the rice. Combine the remaining ingredients in the blender and zip on high for a few seconds. Check for seasoning. Pour the vinaigrette over the rice mixture and check again for seasoning.

Roast Wild Turkey
Fontina Polenta
Fava Beans, Peas, and Pancetta
Green Salad
Rhubarb Tart

Serves four

Although many states now offer a fall turkey hunt this menu is specifically designed for a spring turkey hunt. Both rhubarb and the fava beans are not available fresh except in the spring.

ROAST WILD TURKEY

 1 cup (2 sticks) unsalted butter
 1 tbsp. dried thyme
   Salt and pepper
   Several drops of lemon juice
 1 wild turkey, plucked
   Sprigs of fresh thyme
10 or so bacon strips

Make a compound butter by whipping 1 stick of the unsalted butter. Reconstitute the dried thyme by soaking it in a little hot water and then add it in to the butter. Whip the butter and add salt, pepper, and lemon juice to taste. Refrigerate for 1 hour or overnight. Spread the butter between the skin of the turkey and the meat trying not to tear the skin. Salt and pepper the cavity and stuff with the sprigs of fresh thyme. Truss the turkey and lay the bacon strips over it. Melt the remaining stick of butter, rinse a covering of cheese cloth in water and then soak in the melted butter. Cover the whole bird with it. Roast at 325° for 10 minutes per pound. Baste the turkey with its own juices every ½ hour. If the bird has not browned nicely ½ hour before it is supposed to be done, remove the cheese cloth.

FONTINA POLENTA

1 small onion (optional)
6 tbsp. unsalted butter
2 cups milk
¾ cup cornmeal
5 oz. fontina, diced
½ tsp. nutmeg
1 tsp. kosher salt
½ cup heavy cream
Pepper

If you are using the onion, sauté it in the butter until translucent. Then, in a small saucepan bring the onion, butter and milk to a boil. Add the cornmeal slowly, stirring constantly till thick and the spoon can stand up in it. Be careful as the polenta will spit at you. Now add the cheese, nutmeg and salt. Remove from the heat and beat in the cream and pepper. Turn immediately into buttered muffin tins and let rest till set. Remove from the tin and put in a heavy oven-proof pan and cook at 400° for 15 minutes (if you like, you can add a little more cheese to the tops of the polenta muffins before putting them in the oven.)

FAVA BEANS, PEAS, AND PANCETTA

1 lb. fava beans
4 oz. pancetta
1 box frozen peas, defrosted (Birds Eye Tender Tiny Peas are better than most fresh unless from your own garden, of course.)
Salt, pepper and butter pats

Remove the fava beans from their pods. Peel the outer skin from each bean. This is very tedious and boring but important and worth doing. Steam the beans till barely done, about 5 minutes. Then dip in ice water. Dice the pancetta into ⅛-inch pieces and sauté over a low heat until it is not quite crispy. Remove it from the pan. Rinse the defrosted peas in cool water and drain well. Put the peas and the fava beans into the pan with the pancetta fat and, over a medium flame, heat through. Put into a serving dish, add salt, pepper, pancetta and a little butter and toss.

RHUBARB TART

- ½ lb. pastry of Pepperidge Farm Puff Pastry or your own (or mine, p.250)
- 3 lbs. rhubarb (preferably the young sticks)
- ¾ cup sugar, plus enough to sprinkle on the pastry
- 1 lemon, grated
- Splash of vanilla or sherry
- ⅔ cup crème fraîche or a mixture of sour cream and heavy cream
- 2 tbsp. confectioners' sugar
- ½ tsp. powdered cloves

Roll out the pastry into a buttered 9-inch tart or pastry dish and refrigerate for 1 hour.

With a knife peel the thin outer layer from each stick of rhubarb and slice very thinly. Put in a heavy saucepan with the granulated sugar. Cover and cook 15 minutes over a medium low heat. Then remove the lid and turn the heat up to evaporate all the juices. Stir constantly so it will not stick and burn. Once it has reached the consistency of jam remove and let cool. Add the lemon rind and a few drops of the vanilla or sherry.

Prick the bottom of the refrigerated pastry shell with a fork and place foil tightly over the pastry. Fill with pie weights or beans and cook on the lower shelf of a preheated oven at 425° for 8 minutes. Remove the foil and weights, prick the crust again, sprinkle with a little granulated sugar and return it to the oven for 5 more minutes or until the crust is caramelized and golden. Remove it from the oven and carefully slide the crust onto a cake rack to cool.

Whip the cream and sour cream (or just the crème fraîche) together with the confectioners' sugar and clove. When it's thick, spread it over the bottom of the pastry shell. Then spread the rhubarb over the whipped cream mixture and serve within 30 minutes.

Pheasant in Wine
Fiddleheads
Baked Grits
Strawberry Tart

Serves four

Fiddleheads are spring-time ferns which have not unfolded and look like wheels on the end of a stalk. They can be collected in the woods or, I've noticed, more and more grocery stores are selling them. There is one advantage to buying the store bought ones: the chaff, which I refer to in the recipe, has at least been partially removed. Lest you be too cavalier with this notion I impart the following tale.

Set on always trying to obtain wild food and wanting my children to understand the bounty of the woods, the family set out on an excursion to gather fiddleheads and came home quite successfully with a large basketful. I tried everything I could think of to get the chaff off: From soaking to picking, and finally in desperation I called my friends, the Renesons, who I knew to be fanciers of the vegetable. Unfortunately, Chet answered the phone. When I asked him how to get the moldy-looking stuff off the fiddleheads he suggested the following: In the bow of your Grand Laker canoe place your spouse and the basket of fiddleheads. In the stern, seated at the throttle of the 50-horse Johnson, place yourself dressed in black sou'wester and hat. Once untied from the dock, speed boat at full throttle the length of a 10-mile lake with spouse holding up each individual fiddlehead and you—hopefully—dodging the flying chaff.

Besides finding this method rather impractical, Chet's droll description for how to get rid of the chaff pretty much convinced me of the unreliability in his methodology. However, in the years that have ensued I have been tempted in desperation to at least try it. The chaff is very, very difficult to get off—lots of plunging into boiling water, multiple rinses in cold water, and rubbing it off in a towel—and I suggest leaving all but the cleanest of fiddleheads (collected early in the day and early in the spring) to cover the forest floor.

PHEASANT IN WINE

- 2 pheasants, cut up
- Bacon fat
- 1 carrot
- 1 onion
- ½ celery stalk
- 4 tbsp. unsalted butter
- 1 cup chicken stock
- 1 cup white wine
- 3 tsp. basil
- 1½ tsp. cornstarch, mixed in a tablespoon of water

First brown the pheasant pieces in a little bacon fat. Remove the pheasant from the pan. Dice the carrot, onion, and ½ celery stick into ⅛-inch pieces and sauté them in the pan with the butter. Return all the pheasant pieces but the breasts to the pan, set on top of the vegetables. Add the wine and stock so the pieces are not quite covered. Bring to a simmer and add the basil. Press aluminum foil down on top of the birds so that there is no space between the liquid and the foil and then cover the pan with a lid. Cook about 30 minutes. Add the breasts and cook for an additional 10 minutes.

Put the pheasant pieces onto a warmed platter. Thicken the juices with cornstarch and pour the sauce over the birds just before serving.

FIDDLEHEADS

- 1 lb. fiddleheads
- 3 tbsp. unsalted butter
- Salt and pepper

Cut the bottoms off the fiddleheads leaving about ¾ of the stem. In a large soup pot or bowl full of cold water soak the fiddleheads for 5 minutes or so. Then, by the handful, rinse the fiddleheads under the faucet. Pour out the potful of water and repeat the process two or three more times or until the brown chaff has been completely removed. It is very important to remove as much of the chaff as possible because it causes the fiddleheads to be bitter. Bring a quart of salted water to boil and drop in just a handful of the fiddleheads. Cook for 3 to 4 minutes or until they're just tender. Scoop them out and plunge them into ice water to stop the cooking. Drain the fiddleheads and dry them on an old towel. Repeat this until you have cooked all the .fiddleheads, changing the boiling water with each handful of fiddleheads. Finally, sauté the fiddleheads quickly in the unsalted butter and serve. It's worth it.

BAKED GRITS

- 1½ tsp. salt
- ¾ cup grits
- 3 cups boiling water
- 2 eggs
- ⅛ tsp. cayenne
- ½ lb. grated sharp cheddar cheese
- 4 tbsp. unsalted butter, sliced into thin pats

Add the salt and grits to the boiling water and cook until done or the consistency of bubbling oatmeal. Remove from the heat and let cool slightly then add the eggs one at a time, cayenne, and cheese. Check the seasoning and then place in a buttered baking dish, dot with butter pats, and cook in a preheated oven at 350° for 1 hour.

STRAWBERRY TART

- 1 sheet Pepperidge Farm Puff Pastry or your own (or mine, p.250)
- 1 tbsp. butter for buttering dish
- 2 tbsp. sugar for sprinkling on pastry
- ½ pint heavy cream
- ½ tbsp. Grand Marnier (or your choice of liqueur)
- 3 tbsp. sour cream
- 2 pints strawberries
- 2 tbsp. currant jam

Preheat the oven at 425° for at least 20 minutes.

Roll out the pastry and fit into a porcelain tart or quiche dish heavily buttered. Roll the rolling pin over the top to cut the extra pastry off the edges. Let rest in the refrigerator for 1 hour. Prick the pastry with a fork and then flatten a piece of foil over it. Put beans, peas, or pastry weights on top of the foil. Cook in the lower part of the hot oven for 7 minutes, then carefully open the oven and remove the foil and weights. Sprinkle with sugar and continue cooking for at least 5 minutes until the crust is a light brown with a shiny, caramelized surface. Then remove from the oven and let cool 1 minute. Slide the pastry out of the dish onto a cake rack to cool completely. Whip the cream. About half way through whipping add the Grand Marnier (Framboise is good, too) and the sour cream. Spread over the bottom of the pastry shell. Arrange the strawberries on top of the cream attractively (raspberries, blueberries or any fruit are good also). Melt the currant jam over a low flame. Remove and let cool slightly. To the jam add a dash of the liqueur you used in the cream. Now, with a 2-inch pastry brush, paint the strawberries with the jam mixture. Serve immediately as it will become soggy if you try to hold it more than one hour.

Grilled Quail
Grilled Mushrooms
Purée of Peas
Pear Cake

Serves four

Peas are one of the few vegetables that are just about as good from a frozen package as fresh. Unless you have grown them yourself and picked them yourself and they are young and tiny, then, of course, there is no comparison. But then you shouldn't be wasting them on a purée like this recipe, either.

GRILLED QUAIL

- ¼ lb. pancetta
- 12 crushed juniper berries
- 4 cloves garlic, peeled and crushed
- 4 shallots, peeled and crushed
- 2 bay leaves
- 1 cup white wine
- 4 quail, butterflied (see page 255)
- 1 tbsp. unsalted butter
- 2 tbsp. oil
- Salt and pepper

Dice the pancetta and sauté. When it is about half way cooked add the juniper berries, garlic cloves, shallots, bay leaves and wine. Stir together and then pour over the quail. Cover and refrigerate overnight turning the birds two or three times. Remove from the refrigerator about 1 hour before cooking.

Grill the birds in a little butter and oil, bone side first as always. Cook about 3 minutes per side and baste with the marinade.

GRILLED MUSHROOMS

1 lb. large mushrooms (whole or halved) such as portobello
3 tbsp. unsalted butter
Salt and pepper

Grill the mushrooms for 3-4 minutes and then sauté them in the butter. Season with salt and pepper.

PURÉE OF PEAS

2 lbs. frozen peas
4 tbsp. unsalted butter, cut into pats
½ cup cream
Salt and pepper

Cook the peas in 2 cups of water, covered, till they are tender, about 10 minutes. Drain the peas and push through a strainer. Discard the skins and return the purée to the pan with the butter and cream. Whisk over a low flame for a few seconds until warm. Add salt and pepper to taste.

PEAR CAKE

  2 eggs
¼ cup milk
  2 tsp. vanilla, pear liqueur or rum
  1 cup sugar
     Pinch of salt
     Rind of one orange, grated
1½ cups flour
  2 lbs. fresh pears
     Butter to grease the cake pan
½ cup unflavored bread crumbs

Preheat the oven to 350°. Beat the eggs, milk and vanilla (or liqueur) together in a bowl. Add the sugar, salt and orange rind and continue beating. Now blend in the flour. Peel the pears and cut them in half. Scoop out the seeds and core and slice into pieces no more than 1 inch thick and add to the flour, egg, and sugar mixture. Grease a 9-inch cake pan with butter and then sprinkle finely-ground bread crumbs into it. Shake the crumbs all about and then empty the pan of any excess crumbs. Pour the batter into the cake tin and level it with a spoon. Bake in the preheated oven for 45 minutes or until it is a light brown. Let it cool and then remove it from the pan. The pear cake can be eaten lukewarm or cold. It's good served with a lightly whipped cream, too.

Quick Grilled Quail
Sautéed Watercress
Cauliflower with Mayonnaise
Chocolate Cake

Serves four

Sautéed watercress is wonderful and should be used often.

Using homemade mayonnaise really makes a tremendous difference to the cauliflower and using fancy chocolate versus Baker's less of a difference to the cake even though I say it does. If short on time don't drive to the gourmet shop for the chocolate; make the mayonnaise instead.

QUICK GRILLED QUAIL

4 quail
Several juniper berries per bird
4 strips of bacon

Into each bird insert several juniper berries and then truss. Wrap the bird in a strip of bacon and slide onto a spit. Grill outside or if the rain begins to douse the fire roast in the oven at 350° for 20 minutes.

SAUTÉED WATERCRESS

3 bunches of watercress
3-4 tbsp. butter
Salt and pepper

Take each bunch of watercress and cut into 2-inch lengths (the bunches should be cut approximately into thirds). Sauté the watercress in the hot unsalted butter for a second or two then add the lid for two minutes. Remove the lid and season with salt and pepper and a little more butter and serve.

CAULIFLOWER WITH MAYONNAISE

- 1 head cauliflower
- 1 cup thin mayonnaise (preferably homemade; see page 252). If not homemade thin store-bought with a little heavy cream.
- ½ tsp. prepared mustard
- Chives
- Salt and pepper

Take the leaves off the cauliflower and separate into florets leaving ½- to 1-inch stems on them. Bring several quarts of water to boil and drop the cauliflower in by handfuls. When the cauliflower is just tender remove from the boiling water and plunge into a iced bath. After it is cooled, drain. Season the mayonnaise mixed with mustard, chives, and salt and pepper and pour over the cauliflower. Toss and serve.

CHOCOLATE CAKE

- ½ lb. (2 sticks) unsalted butter
- ½ lb. unsweetened chocolate (the better the chocolate, the better the cake)
- 1 tbsp. lemon juice
- 2 tbsp. orange liqueur (Cointreau)
- 1 tbsp. vanilla
- 10 eggs, separated
- 1½ cups sugar
- Pinch of salt
- Sprinkle of confectioners' sugar

Butter and flour a 10-inch spring form pan. Cut a 10-inch round of parchment paper and butter and flour that, placing it on the bottom of the spring form pan.

Combine the butter and chocolate in a saucepan and melt both over a low flame. Stir in the lemon juice, liqueur and vanilla. Remove from the heat. Separate the eggs and beat together the egg yolks and sugar until they ribbon lightly and then combine with the chocolate mixture. Beat the egg whites until they just support a whole raw egg without sinking, but are not too stiff. Then stir in ⅓ of the whites into the chocolate mixture. Fold in the remaining whites.

Pour the cake batter into the pan and bake in a preheated oven of 250° for 2½ hours. Turn off the oven and leave the cake in there for 30 minutes. Remove from the oven and let cool completely. Slide a knife around the cake pan, invert on a plate, and release the spring form pan. Remove the paper carefully and sprinkle with confectioners' sugar.

Pheasant Salad
Soup in a Pumpkin
Basil Bread
Figs in Rum

Serves four

PHEASANT SALAD

2-3 pheasants
2 tbsp. butter
1 cup heavy cream
1 tsp. basil
 Salt and pepper
1 can (14 oz.) artichoke hearts (in water/brine)
½ cup olive oil
1 tsp. mustard
2 tbsp. vinegar
½ garlic clove (finely chopped)
 Lettuce

Breast out the pheasants and oven poach them by doing the following: Melt the butter in a fry pan and then quickly toss the breasts in the butter until they are just becoming white on the outside and then place them in a buttered baking dish. Cut a piece of parchment paper to fit the top, butter it, and press it over the pheasant. Bake for 5 minutes in a preheated oven at 450° or until the meat is just springy to the touch. Remember that all meat, but especially the high-in-protein game, continues to cook, often as much as by ⅓ more, after it has been removed from the heat. Now remove the breasts from the pan and skim off any fat in the juice and set the juice aside.

Meanwhile reduce the cream: Over a high heat bring the cream to a boil. Reduce to a simmer. Add basil, salt and pepper and stir every now and then so it doesn't stick to the pan. Cook until it is halved in quantity and thick. Mix in the juices left over from cooking the pheasant and let cool. Slice the pheasant breasts on the diagonal.

Drain the artichoke hearts and soak them in cold water. Change the water 2-3 times to remove the metallic taste from the artichokes which they got from being in the can. Cut into quarters.

Except for the lettuce, combine the remaining ingredients in the blender for 30 seconds or so to make vinaigrette. Mix the vinaigrette with the reduced cream and pheasant juices and pour over the artichokes and pheasant pieces. Toss and check for salt and pepper. Serve on lettuce with French bread.

SOUP IN A PUMPKIN

1 perfect little pumpkin which will fit in your oven and weighs about 6 lbs.
½ cup (1 stick) unsalted butter
1 onion, chopped
5 cups chicken stock
  Bay leaf
  Several parsley stems
  Salt and pepper
½ cup cream
  Croutons
  Chopped parsley

Scoop out the pumpkin. Discard the seeds and string and save the flesh. Be sure not to scoop too close to the skin. Cut the pumpkin flesh into small chunks and sauté it in the butter along with the onion until the pumpkin is soft. Add the stock, bay leaf, and parsley stems. Season with salt and pepper and let cook until the mixture is quite soft. Remove bay leaf. Purée in the blender or a food processor and then strain. Add the cream and check for seasoning. Return the pumpkin soup to the pumpkin shell and cook in the oven for 40 minutes at 350°. Garnish with the croutons and chopped parsley and serve scraping the pumpkin shell sides as you ladle the soup into the bowls.

BASIL BREAD

- 2 cups lukewarm to warm water
- 1 tbsp. dry yeast
- 1 tbsp. sugar
- 1 tbsp. salt
- 2 tbsp. dried basil
- 5 cups or so of all-purpose flour (I recommend King Arthur Flour)
- Butter and oil for greasing pans

In the bowl of a standing mix master, fitted with a bread hook, add the warm water and sprinkle in the yeast, sugar, salt, and basil. Let sit for a few minutes until the yeast looks dissolved and foamy. Now pour in 5 cups of flour and mix at the lowest setting, usually marked "stir," until the flour is blended and then increase the speed to the next level, #2. Continue blending at this speed until the dough is well mixed, pulling away from the sides of the bowl, and forming a ball. Turn onto a floured surface and knead the dough for about 8 minutes. It should be slightly tacky to the touch but smooth and very malleable. Place in a bowl that has been oiled, turn the dough over in the oil so the top is oiled, too, and cover the bowl with a cloth. Let rise until it is double in size, about 2 to 3 hours. Punch it down and let it rest while you prepare the pan(s) for it to rise in again.

This recipe makes enough for a baguette and a loaf. I always make a baguette for the week's spaghetti night so I pull a handful of dough off and roll it into a big snake and lay it in one side of a baguette pan that has been buttered. The remaining dough I either place into a buttered loaf pan, pushing it into the rectangle shape, or form a ball with the dough, flouring it heavily, and put into a banneton, also heavily floured. Both the baguette and the loaf/round I cover with a cloth and let rise again for another hour or so.

The breads in the metal baking pans can go directly into a preheated oven at 420° for 35 to 40 minutes until golden brown. The banneton is trickier. I use a piece of parchment paper, floured, atop the back of a cookie sheet and careful invert the banneton and let the dough fall out. Often it loses its rise and I let it sit covered for another hour to rise again. Once the round is ready to bake I slide it onto a pizza stone that is in a preheated oven at 420° and bake it for 40 minutes or until golden. Once baked, I turn the baguette and loaf out of their pans—or slide the round on the parchment onto the cookie sheet—and onto a rack to cool. Let cool for 30 minutes or so before cutting.

If I don't plan to use the baguette that day I wrap it in foil and put it in the freezer to use another day. (It just needs to be taken from the freezer and put in a preheated oven at 350º for 30 minutes or so.)

FIGS IN RUM

- 2 lbs. fresh figs
- 1 cup sugar
- 1 cup water
- 1 vanilla bean or pinch of thyme or a sprig of fresh thyme
- 4 tbsp. rum
- 1 cup heavy cream

Wash and drain the figs. Simmer the sugar and water together for 5 minutes then add the figs and vanilla bean. Cook slowly over a low heat for 1 hour. Remove from the heat and let cool. Add the rum and cover the fruit tightly, Let it all sit in the refrigerator for 2 days, Whip the cream and serve on top of the figs.

Pheasant and Cabbage
Cooked Apples
Cheese

Serves four

I are very lucky to live near a wonderful apple farm which maintains a wide variety of antique (or "uncommon" as the grower calls them) apple trees. The grower lovingly lists on little individual cards for his customers each apple, its unique characteristics, history, and how the apple should be used. It would be nice to refer you to a specific type of cooking apple for this recipe but it's probably a bit provincial to do so. I do recommend making inquires to local grocers or orchard owners as to what are the best cooking apples in your area to buy.

PHEASANT AND CABBAGE

- 2 whole pheasants, plucked and ready for roasting
- Fresh herbs (or dried)
- 4 thin slices of pancetta
- ½ head of red cabbage
- ½ head of green cabbage
- 2 tbsp. unsalted butter
- Salt and pepper
- Caraway seeds

To prepare the pheasants, stuff the cavity of each bird with the fresh herbs and truss. Wrap each pheasant in pancetta or regular bacon and roast at 350° for 30 minutes. Remove the bacon and cook for an additional 15 or 20 minutes till the birds are brown. While the birds are cooking prepare the cabbage. Halve and then quarter each cabbage and cut off the stiff core. Slice thinly as if for coleslaw. Sauté the cabbage, each color separately, quickly in butter till cooked but still crunchy. Season with salt, pepper and a light dose of caraway. Place the birds on a warmed platter and arrange the cabbage in rings around the birds.

COOKED APPLES

    3 tbsp. unsalted butter
    4 apples (If a New Englander, try the uncommon Calville Blanc d'Hiver or Esopus Spitzenberg. But Baldwin or Cortlands work too.)
    1 tbsp. calvados
    ¼ cup cream
    Salt and pepper

Make noisette butter by melting the butter over a medium-high heat in a frying pan until the butter has turned a light brown (remember it continues to darken after it is taken from the heat). Meanwhile peel and dice the apples. Cook them in the butter until just tender on a medium heat. Turn the heat to high, add the calvados and let the heat evaporate it. Pour in the cream and cook a few minutes until the cream has thickened. Season with salt and pepper.

Woodcock Armagnac on Garlic Toasts
Fennel and Peas
Roast Potatoes
Tarte Tatin

Serves four

When I first wrote this book, I said, "Woodcock are perhaps my least favorite upland bird." Now, 25 years later, it is absolutely my most favorite. Why? For two reasons: It is so unusual, so wild, and the taste of woodcock cannot even come close to that of any other bird, wild or not. It is exceptional and rare in its flavor. Plus, like all great wild edibles, woodcock summon wonderful memories of good times in the woods with my hunting buddies, both two legged and those with four.

When I don't include a specific recipe for something listed in the menu—as in this case with the roast potatoes—it is because I assume you know how to cook it and have a favorite method of doing so. Or in some cases because it requires no cooking at all.

WOODCOCK ARMAGNAC ON GARLIC TOASTS

- 8 slices of French bread
- 2 garlic cloves cut in half
- 5 tbsp. good green olive oil
- 8 woodcock
- 2 tbsp. hot butter
- 3 tbsp. Armagnac
- ½ cup heavy cream
- Salt, pepper, lemon juice or mustard

Rub each of the slices of French bread with garlic and then fry quickly in olive oil until golden. Breast out the woodcock. Sauté the breasts in the hot butter very fast (about 1 minute) and then remove and place two breasts on each slice of fried French bread. Add the Armagnac to the juices left in the pan and stir with a wire whisk making sure to scrape the bottom. Now add the cream and cook on a high heat till thick and reduced to about half the original quantity. Season with salt and pepper and a little mustard or a few drops of lemon juice if you need more tartness. Pour over the breasts and serve.

FENNEL AND PEAS

2 heads fennel, halved and cored
2 tbsp. unsalted butter
1 box frozen peas, defrosted (Birds Eye Tender Tiny Peas are the best)
Salt and pepper

Peel the outer stalks of the fennel with a potato peeler. Julienne all the stalks into ⅛-inch pieces cutting against the grain of the fennel. Sauté the fennel in butter for several minutes till it is tender but not limp. Now add the box of defrosted peas and heat through. Add salt and pepper to taste.

TARTE TATIN

- 6 hard cooking apples (uncommon apples like Calville Blanc d'Hiver or Esopus Spitzenberg are my favorite for this recipe, but Baldwin or Cortlands work too)
- ¾ cup sugar, plus a sprinkle
- ½ cup water
- 2 tbsp. unsalted butter
- Sprinkle of cinnamon
- 1 sheet Pepperidge Farm Puff Pastry, or your own pastry, (or mine, p.250)
- Lightly whipped cream

Peel and slice the apples thinly. Next caramelize the sugar by cooking the water and ¾ cup sugar in a frying pan until it is light brown. Remove immediately from the heat as it will continue to cook and transfer to a cake tin. Spread the caramelized sugar over the bottom and lay the apple slices in concentric circles on top. Only the first layer will show so be sure to make that your best. Dot each layer with butter and sprinkle with sugar and cinnamon. Once the pan is full roll out the pastry and cover the apples with it. Cut a few tiny holes in the pastry to let the steam escape. Cook in the middle of a preheated oven at 450° for 20 minutes. Then turn the heat down to 350° and continue to cook for 30 to 40 minutes. Remove and let cool for a few minutes and then invert onto a serving plate. If it has hardened too much, put the cake tin on a burner and re-melt the caramel. Then invert.

You can add a bit of the extra juices that may run out, once cooled, to the lightly whipped cream.

Chukar Stuffed with Hazelnuts
Grated Zucchini
Sautéed Cherry Tomatoes
Cheese, Thyme Toast
Fresh Fruit

Serves four

CHUKAR STUFFED WITH HAZELNUTS

- 4 chukars, skinned
- ⅓ cup toasted and finely chopped hazelnuts
- ¼ cup bread crumbs, sifted fine
- 1 tbsp. parsley, chopped fine
- Salt and pepper
- Pinch of thyme
- 2 tbsp. cream (for moistening)
- 3 tbsp. unsalted butter

Cut the breasts off the bone. Roast the hazelnuts in the oven, steam in a tea towel and remove skins. To chop them fine, you can use a food processor. Combine the hazelnuts with the bread crumbs, 1 teaspoon of the parsley, salt and pepper, a pinch of thyme and some cream to moisten it all. Make a slice on the keel-bone edge of each breast and stuff with the nut mixture. Oven poach the breasts by doing the following: Quickly toss the breasts in 2 tablespoons of melted butter. When the breasts are just turning white remove them and put into a buttered baking dish. Cut a piece of parchment paper to fit the top, butter it and press it over the chukar breasts. Bake for 15 minutes in a preheated oven at 400° or until the meat is just springy to the touch. Slice the breast on the diagonal in three pieces and arrange attractively on a platter. Lightly brown the remaining butter in a small pan and add any juices from the poaching pan. Dribble this over the top of the breasts and sprinkle with the remaining parsley chopped fine. Season with salt and pepper.

GRATED ZUCCHINI

    4 medium zucchini
       Salt
    1 lb. spinach
    1 shallot, chopped
    2 tbsp. unsalted butter
       Salt and pepper

Grate the zucchini coarsely. Put it in a strainer and sprinkle with salt. Let stand and drain for 20 minutes. Meanwhile wash the spinach, shake dry, and barely wilt it over a medium-low flame with the lid on for a second. Drain the spinach, let cool, then chop. Squeeze the water out of the zucchini. Sauté the shallot in butter over a medium heat and add the zucchini to it. Add the spinach. Stirring continuously, heat the vegetables over medium heat till hot to the touch. Add salt and pepper to taste and serve.

SAUTÉED CHERRY TOMATOES

    24 cherry tomatoes
    2 tbsp. unsalted butter
       Several sprigs of fresh basil (or any other fresh
         herb you may have; dried herbs work, too)
       Salt and pepper

Prick each cherry tomato with a pin to prevent the tomato skins from bursting and remove the green tops. Sauté in the butter till hot and sprinkle with the chopped herb and salt and pepper. Serve.

CHEESE, THYME TOAST

   1 loaf French bread
  ¼ cup olive oil
  ½ lb. gruyere cheese
      Sprinkles of dried thyme
      Salt
      Hot pepper flakes

Slice the bread and grill it, toasting it lightly. Brush each piece with oil and lay a piece of cheese on top. Sprinkle the thyme, salt and pepper flakes on top and broil till the cheese just bubbles.

Water Fowl

My hunting and fishing, as with many folks, has gone through different stages. Thirty years ago we lived on a Massachusetts marsh, had a golden retriever, had 12-gauge side-by-sides and could shoot three black ducks a day, which we tried to take advantage of nearly every day of the season. Now we live in the hills of New Hampshire and have a pointing dog. I hunt grouse and woodcock with a little 26-inch over-and-under 20-gauge and spend a week in Canada to help insure the winter's woodcock feast. We rarely hunt ducks, and then only on the Connecticut River, but the lack of an appropriate dog and the relatively limited number of birds make the attempt a bit half-hearted.

But I miss duck hunting. So it was with great glee we accepted an invitation to hunt for black ducks with a friend and his toller dog, out of duck blinds in the Grand Lake area of New Brunswick. As an added benefit, it was to be part of a magazine story and our photographer friend, Tom Montgomery, would do the photography.

One of my favorite aspects of duck hunting is the long space of time that's given over to sweet anticipation. That first morning's return to duck hunting brought back all the great memories: Wadered bodies, thermoses of hot coffee; guns and dogs in boats; dark and cold and whistle of wings; pale, gray dawn and pink-tinged clouds peeking into the blind as you peek out. Then it's time; they're coming, they're coming, they're almost here.

Now stand, shoot and watch the retrieve: It's spectacular! Well, maybe it's just wonderful.

Tom hadn't photographed a duck hunt before and he was reveling in the visual beauty of the scene. Clicking, clicking away he photographed everything. *Everything!* I realized with a sudden self-consciousness. I was dressed in so many layers of wool, goose-down and rubber that I could easily have been mistaken for the Pillsbury doughboy's bigger camo-clad cousin. And as Tom focused in on that close-up facial shot that shows the eager anticipation (and fortunately loses the dough-boy body) did he have to point out that my red nose had something dripping from it—after he'd shot the last five frames of film? Now wait, this was not focused and hunter-like. Tom had photographed me before hunting and fishing and the photos had always come out wonderfully. And of course these did, too. Either through darkroom magic or careful editing Tom made me, even in duck hunting regalia, look attractive and real. What a wizard he is.

Do looks really matter? Probably not with ducks on the marsh and that only in order to identify what species are legal to shoot But actually I do believe that duck appearances—not species—can make a big difference in the kitchen.

Most game cookbooks list duck recipes by species. I've not done that here. It took me a long time to learn that although it's tremendously important to know the differences between species when *hunting* ducks, what species it is makes very little difference once the duck is inside the kitchen. What is important are the variations in diet, age, what kind of weather the specific duck has experienced, how it was treated in the field and its overall size. In general, an older, larger duck is tougher than a young small one. In general, a late-season duck that has already endured a period of limited food and hard weather will have a less appealing flavor. And of course, whether the duck has been cleanly shot and carefully dressed will affect the taste, too. (See the chapter on "Game Care" for more details.) What a game cook needs to develop is a sense of how to cook the bird according to how it looks rather than how to prepare it based on it being a mallard or a black duck. A fleshy, pale-skinned duck with no tears in the skin and all blood and fat deposits properly removed will simply taste better.

There are two broad but critical differences that do affect the cooking and thus the choice of recipe. So I've indicated when the recipe should be used for sea ducks and also, the general size of the duck that the recipe calls for. The suggested sea duck recipes are based on how much you might prefer to mask some of the fishy taste that often taints sea duck or a duck that becomes a fish-eater in the late-season. The indication on size is to give you some idea of how the temperature and allotted time were determined for cooking the duck. Any of the recipes are applicable to any species of duck and you should just take into account what was in mind—the duck's size and diet—when the recipe was being designed.

Duck with Ginger and Scallions
Sautéed Watercress
Cheese, Thyme Toast
Chocolate Cake

Serves four

DUCK WITH GINGER AND SCALLIONS

- 4 ducks, breasted out
- 4 tbsp. hot unsalted butter
- 1 bunch of scallions
- 1 2-inch piece of ginger root
- ¼ cup sesame oil
- 1 cup stock

Slice the duck breasts horizontally in half and sauté in 1 tablespoon of the butter for 3-4 minutes per side or until springy to the touch.

Chop the green part of the scallions into ¼-inch pieces. Peel and julienne the ginger into pieces ¹⁄₁₆ by 1 inch in size and put into a little cup with some sesame oil.

Put the cooked duck breasts onto a heated platter. Add the stock to the pan that the ducks were cooked in and cook over a high heat scraping the bottom with a wire whisk. Cook until the liquid has been reduced to ¼ cup. Whisk in the remaining 3 tablespoons of butter. Now add the ginger and scallions. Arrange the ducks attractively on the warmed platter and pour the sauce over them. Serve.

SAUTÉED WATERCRESS

- 3 bunches of watercress
- 3-4 tbsp. unsalted butter
- Salt and pepper

Take each bunch of watercress and cut into 2-inch lengths (the bunches should be cut approximately into thirds). Sauté the watercress in the hot unsalted butter for a second or two then add the lid for two minutes. Remove the lid, season with salt and pepper and a little more butter, and serve.

CHEESE, THYME TOAST

- 1 loaf French bread
- ¼ cup olive oil
- ½ lb. gruyere cheese
- Sprinkles of dried thyme
- Salt
- Hot pepper flakes

Slice the bread and grill or toast it until it is golden. Brush each piece with oil and lay a piece of cheese on top. Sprinkle the thyme, salt and pepper flakes on top and broil till the cheese just bubbles.

CHOCOLATE CAKE

- ½ lb. (2 sticks) unsalted butter
- ½ lb. unsweetened chocolate (the better the chocolate, the better the cake)
- 1 tbsp. lemon juice
- 2 tbsp. orange liqueur (Cointreau)
- 1 tbsp. vanilla
- 10 eggs, separated
- 1½ cups sugar
- Pinch of salt
- Sprinkle of confectioners' sugar

Butter and flour a 10-inch spring form pan. Cut a 10-inch round of parchment paper and butter and flour that, placing it on the bottom of the spring form pan.

Combine the butter and chocolate in a saucepan and melt both over a low flame. Stir in the lemon juice, liqueur and vanilla. Remove from the heat. Separate the eggs and beat together the egg yolks and sugar until they ribbon lightly and then combine with the chocolate mixture. Beat the egg whites until they just support a whole raw egg without sinking, but are not too stiff. Then stir in ⅓ of the whites into the chocolate mixture. Fold in the remaining whites.

Pour the cake batter into the pan and bake in a preheated oven at 250° for 2½ hours. Turn off the oven and leave the cake in there for 30 minutes. Remove from the oven and let cool completely. Slide a knife around the cake pan, invert on a plate, and release the spring form pan. Remove the paper carefully and sprinkle with confectioners' sugar.

Ducks with Rosemary and Sage
Fontina Polenta
Zucchini Fans with Tomatoes
Coffee Ice Cream with Hazelnut Liqueur

Serves four

Fresh herbs can make a tremendous difference, particularly when not much else is happening in the recipe. However, fresh herbs sometimes can be difficult to buy during hunting season. I suggest buying little thyme plants or whatever, using them heavily throughout hunting season, and throwing them out when the leaves have all been used or you forget to water it. Don't worry about trying to preserve the plant for some magnificent herbal garden. Use it, throw it out, and buy more. But do use it.

This recipe would be good for ducks in the size-range of mallards, pintails or black ducks.

The state where we lived until 1989, Massachusetts, claimed that there were more ice cream parlors there than in any other state in the country. Consequently, it was always easy for us to slip down to the local parlor and buy their freshly made ice cream. Even if you live where they have more gas stations than any other state—and the ice cream has been in the cooler there since before cars—you'll still find this is a delightful and easy dessert. Unlike some flavors, coffee ice cream seems to be generally good from any source and doesn't need to be particularly fresh. The addition of hazelnut liqueur makes it ooh la la.

DUCKS WITH ROSEMARY AND SAGE

- 2 tbsp. rosemary
- 3 tbsp. sage
- 2 tbsp. salt
- 2 tbsp. pepper
- 1 cup duck and chicken livers chopped fine
- 1 small onion
- 2 roasting ducks
- 4 strips bacon
- 4 cups stock
- 2 tbsp. cognac
- 3 tbsp. butter

Hopefully the rosemary and sage are fresh; if so chop fine. Add to the salt and pepper. Chop the livers and add to the finely chopped onion. Take half the herb mixture and add it to the onions and livers. Stuff the onion, liver, and herbs into the cavity of each duck and truss. Rub the remaining half of the herb mixture over the skin and add two strips of bacon on to each bird. Roast at 350° for 40 minutes. Remove the bacon and brown for 10 more minutes. Place the ducks onto a heated platter.

Reduce the stock to two cups.

Deglaze a pan with cognac and add the reduced stock. Now remove the livers from the ducks and add it to the stock. Whisk in the butter while heating the liver mixture over low heat. Carve the ducks and pour a little of the sauce over the meat.

FONTINA POLENTA

- 1 small onion (optional)
- 6 tbsp. unsalted butter
- 2 cups milk
- ¾ cup cornmeal
- 5 oz. fontina, diced
- ½ tsp. nutmeg
- 1 tsp. kosher salt
- ½ cup heavy cream
- Pepper

If you are using the onion, sauté it in the butter until translucent. Then, in a small saucepan bring the onion, butter and milk to a boil. Add the cornmeal slowly, stirring constantly till thick and the spoon can stand up in it. Be careful as the polenta will spit at you. Now add the cheese, nutmeg and salt. Remove from the heat and beat in the cream and pepper. Turn immediately into buttered muffin tins and let rest till set. Remove from the tin and put in a heavy oven-proof pan and cook at 400° for 15 minutes (if you like, you can add a little more cheese to the tops of the polenta muffins before putting them in the oven.)

ZUCCHINI FANS WITH TOMATOES

- 6 small zucchini
- 4 small tomatoes
- Fresh basil
- 3 tbsp. unsalted butter
- Salt and pepper

Make four deep cuts from top to bottom into each zucchini, slicing almost to the base and creating a fan out of each zucchini. Slice the tomatoes and slip them into the zucchini cuts. Arrange carefully in a buttered baking dish and sprinkle with basil. Dot with butter and bake in a 350° oven for 20 minutes or until tender. Place in a serving dish with a spatula and season with salt and pepper.

Grilled Sea Ducks
Grilled Vegetables
Garlic Cheese Bread
Poached Pears

Serves four

GRILLED SEA DUCKS

- 1 loaf of day-old French bread
- 3 cloves of garlic sliced in half
- 2-3 tbsp. bacon or pancetta fat
- ¼ cup (½ stick) unsalted butter
- 4 sea ducks, breasted out

Slice the French bread and rub each side of the slices with the garlic. Sauté the bread in the bacon fat and butter and let cool. Crumble the bread and set aside.

Grill the breasts over a medium hot fire for 3-4 minutes per side. Sprinkle the breasts with the bread crumbs and season with salt and pepper.

GRILLED VEGETABLES

- 2 red peppers
- 1 eggplant, sliced and sprinkled with salt
- 1 zucchini
- 1 yellow squash
- 3 tbsp. unsalted butter, melted
- Salt and pepper

Roast the red peppers on the grill, turning them till each side gets black. Remove and let cool. Peel off the black skin. Remove the seeds and cut into 1-inch slivers.

Slice the eggplant into ¼-inch thick pieces. Sprinkle both sides of each piece with salt and let stand and drain for 30 minutes. Grill till the grill marks show on each side.

Cut the zucchini and yellow squash into ¼-inch slices and grill until the marks show.

Toss the four vegetables together and sauté in hot butter over a medium heat. Add salt and pepper to taste.

GARLIC CHEESE BREAD

- 8 slices of French bread
- 1 garlic clove, cut in half
- 3 oz. fontina
- 3 oz. mozzarella
- Pepper

Slice the French bread and rub each piece with the peeled garlic clove. Toast under the broiler. Sliver the fontina and the mozzarella and sprinkle on top of the toast. Run them under the broiler for a minute or two and then season with salt and pepper.

POACHED PEARS

- 4 ripe pears
- Several drops of lemon juice
- 2 cups water
- 1⅓ cups sugar
- 1 vanilla bean, split

Peel the pears with a vegetable peeler and core from the bottom with a melon bailer. Rub the peeled pears with lemon juice. In a saucepan combine water, a few drops of lemon juice, and sugar and bring it to a boil. Add the halved vanilla bean and reduce the heat. Simmer for 5 minutes. Then add the pears and continue to simmer for about 10 minutes or until the pears are tender. Remove the pears from the syrup and stand upright on a plate in the refrigerator. The chilled pears can be served with crème anglaise, whipped cream, chocolate shavings, or a liqueur over it.

Grilled Breast of Mallard
Gorgonzola Polenta
Cucumber and Radishes
Fresh Fruit

Serves four

Okay, I broke my rule about not specifying a species of duck in a recipe. But this recipe is very much designed for a mallard, particularly a mallard that's been spending time away from the ocean. I've always been a staunch supporter of the blacks and mallards that live by the sea and honestly believe there is very little difference in taste from those that feast on corn each day; but there is one thing that makes an inland mallard special—the skin. For some reason these ducks have especially good tasting skin. It does seem unfortunate to go to the trouble of plucking a duck just to breast it out, but the skin sautéed separately is delicious—and best if it's one of those corn-fed mallards.

I'd also recommend this recipe for use on a duck hunting camping trip.

GRILLED BREAST OF MALLARD

4 mallards
3-4 tbsp. pancetta or bacon fat

After the ducks have been plucked, skin them and cut the breasts out. Save the skin and pound the breasts to ¼ inch thickness and paint with melted bacon fat.

Cut the skin into strips—this can be done either with poultry sheers or scissors—and sautéed in the fat till crispy (about 20 minutes). Chop and set aside.

Grill the breasts over a medium hot fire, about 3 minutes a side. Sprinkle the pieces of skin over the breasts and serve.

GORGONZOLA POLENTA

1 small onion chopped fine (optional)
2 cups milk
6 tbsp. unsalted butter
¾ cup cornmeal
5 oz. gorgonzola, diced
½ tsp. nutmeg
1 tsp. kosher salt
½ cup heavy cream
Pepper to taste

If you are using the onion, sauté it in the butter until translucent.

Then, in a small saucepan, bring the onion, milk, and butter to a boil. Add the cornmeal slowly, stirring constantly till thick and the spoon can stand up in it. Be careful as the polenta will spit at you. Remove from the heat and add the cheese, nutmeg, salt, cream and pepper and mix well. Turn immediately into buttered muffin tins and let rest till set. Remove from the tin and put in a heavy oven-proof pan and cook at 400° for 15 minutes (if you like, you can add a little more cheese to the tops of the polenta muffins before putting them in the oven.)

CUCUMBERS AND RADISHES

1 bunch radishes
2 cucumbers
2 tbsp. unsalted butter
Mint or dill
Salt and pepper

Clean and slice the radishes thickly (⅛-inch thick). Peel the cucumbers then cut them in half the long way. Scoop out the seeds and then slice each half into ⅛-inch pieces. Sauté the cucumbers and radishes in the butter. Season with salt and pepper and a little mint or dill.

Stuffed Duck Breasts
Green Beans with Wild Mushrooms
Bibb and Radish Salad
Grapefruit Sabayon

Serves four

My preference in general is to pluck and roast a duck. This is not always desirable, however, if it is quite shot up or the skin has torn for some other reason. This recipe is for just such a dilapidated duck.

Fortunately, dried wild mushrooms can be purchased in nice little plastic bags these days. There certainly is no need to risk life and psyche by trying to collect them if you are an inexperienced forager.

STUFFED DUCK BREASTS

- 1 lb. spinach
- ¼ cup currants, soaked in a little Armagnac
- ¼ cup stock
- 1 egg
- ¾ cup bread crumbs
- 1 tsp. tarragon
- 1 tbsp. fresh, chopped basil
- Salt and pepper
- 4 ducks, breasted out
- 5 tbsp. unsalted butter

Wash the spinach and put it in a pan with a tight lid over a medium heat for a few minutes until the spinach is just barely limp. Let cool and then chop. Combine the spinach with the currants and their juices, the stock, the egg, the bread crumbs, the tarragon, the basil, and salt and pepper to taste. Cut a pocket in each duck breast and stuff the spinach mixture into the breast. Oven poach the breasts by sautéing them in half the butter for just a few minutes. Place In a buttered baking dish and cut a round of parchment paper to fit over the top of the dish and butter it. Press the paper over the breasts. Cook for 15 minutes at 400° or until the meat is springy to the touch.

Make a noisette butter by heating the remaining amount of butter until it turns a hazelnut brown. Pour over the breasts. Season with salt and pepper.

GREEN BEANS WITH WILD MUSHROOMS

    1 lb. green beans
    1 oz. dried wild mushrooms
    2 tbsp. unsalted butter
    Salt and pepper

Blanch the green beans and then chill them immediately in ice water. Reconstitute the mushrooms in a little warm water. Rinse the mushrooms in cool water saving the reconstituted juice. Reduce a little of the juice in a sauté pan (be sure not to get any of the mushrooms' grit in the pan) until it is just a glaze on the bottom of the pan. Melt the butter with the glaze and add the mushrooms and beans. Sauté, then season with salt and pepper.

GRAPEFRUIT SABAYON

    2 pink grapefruits
    2 white grapefruits
    3 egg yolks
    ½ cup sugar
    ½ cup wine or rum
    Pinch of salt
    1 tbsp. Grand Marnier

Cut the peel off of the grapefruits making sure to remove all of the white pith. Then slice into rounds and core and seed each round. Arrange attractively in an oven-proof dish.

Make the sabayon by first beating the egg yolks and sugar together until it lightly ribbons. Add the wine and a pinch of salt. Over a medium-low heat (the pan should never get too hot on the bottom to touch) whisk constantly to incorporate air into the egg, sugar and wine mixture. Once it's thickened blend in the liqueur or lemon juice and pour the sabayon over the grapefruit. Run the dessert under the broiler for a few minutes to just brown the surface.

Duck Salad
Basil Pasta
Cantaloupe Ice

Serves four

Sun-dried tomatoes, listed in the next recipe, are no longer very difficult to find—as they were when I first wrote this book in 1982. Most often found in grocery stores or in gourmet shops in canisters like any other dried fruit, sun-dried tomatoes also are available packed in oil at a higher cost. They are wonderful and worth it in either form.

When making vinaigrette it's nice to know that a mistake of too much vinegar or lemon can be corrected by adding a little more salt.

Homemade pasta is wonderful, although it can be tedious to make (see page 43) and definitely would be wasted in this recipe. The imported boxed pasta is suited to heavy sauces and vinaigrettes and can be purchased in delightful shapes.

Try to use a very ripe cantaloupe for the ice recipe.

DUCK SALAD

- 4 ducks, roasted
- 2 apples
- 8 slices bacon
- ¾ cup sun-dried tomatoes
- 2 cloves garlic
- Bouquet garni (bay leaf, parsley stems, thyme)
- A few peppercorns
- 1 tsp. fennel seeds
- ⅓ cup olive oil
- ⅓ cup white wine
- ½ lb. snow peas
- 2 scallions
- ½ tbsp. vinegar
- ¼ tsp. prepared mustard
- Salt and pepper

To roast the four ducks stuff each with half an apple and then truss it. Lay two strips of bacon on each duck and roast in a 350° oven for 50 minutes. Let the ducks cool and then remove the meat from the bones.

Next reconstitute the sun-dried tomatoes. In a small pot combine the peeled garlic cloves, tomatoes, bouquet garni, peppercorns, a few crushed fennel seeds and the olive oil and white wine. Simmer over a low heat until the tomatoes are soft (about 15 minutes). Let cool and dice. Be sure to save the oil and white wine mixture for making the dressing. Add the tomatoes to the pieces of duck meat.

Blanch the snow peas in a large quantity of salted, boiling water for about 30 seconds. Remove from the water and plunge into ice water to maintain the green color. Drain and dry and add to the duck and tomatoes.

Chop the green part of the scallions and add it to the salad with the crushed fennel seeds.

Make a dressing by putting into the blender the juice from the reconstituted tomatoes, the vinegar, and the mustard. Blend on high for 10 seconds. Taste for seasoning and correct. Pour over the duck combination and toss.

BASIL PASTA

- 1 cup olive oil
- 2 large cloves garlic
- 1 bay leaf
- ⅓ cup vinegar
- Touch of lemon juice
- 1 tbsp. prepared mustard
- Salt and pepper
- 1 large bunch fresh basil
- 1 lb. pasta
- Hot pepper flakes
- 6 oz. goat cheese, crumbled

In the cup of olive oil cook the peeled garlic cloves over a medium-low heat for about 20 minutes or until the garlic is soft but still holds its shape. Add the bay leaf while it is still hot and let sit overnight.

Make a little vinaigrette with the vinegar, lemon juice, mustard, and salt and pepper. Pour the vinaigrette into a blender and add the basil with the stems removed and the olive oil garlic (less the bay leaf). Blend till smooth. Check for seasoning.

Cook the pasta particularly *al dente* (it will absorb the moisture from the basil mixture and become mushy if cooked till soft). Drain the pasta, cool a little (or it will discolor the basil vinaigrette and make its brilliant green appearance not so attractive) and toss with the basil vinaigrette. Sprinkle with red pepper flakes and crumbled goat cheese. Decorate with any extra little basil leaves.

CANTALOUPE ICE

2 very ripe cantaloupes
¾ cup confectioners' sugar
A pinch of salt
Lemon juice to taste
1 tbsp. white rum
(Make sure you have enough ice and salt for your ice cream machine)

Halve the cantaloupes and scoop out the seeds. Now scoop out the fruit and make sure you have about 1 quart. Purée the cantaloupe in a blender and then add the sugar, salt, and lemon juice sparingly until the mixture tastes right. Now add the rum and make any adjustments for taste. Place the cantaloupe mixture in the canister of your ice cream machine and place in the refrigerator for a couple of hours. Then freeze it in the machine according to the manufacturer's directions. For a nice effect you can pack the ice cream back into the cantaloupe shells.

Grilled Marinated Ducks
Grilled Red Onion
Grilled Mushrooms
Basil Bread
Crème Brulée

Serves four

All of the bread recipes in this book are based on a basic white bread recipe which originated from the back of a King Arthur flour bag. It's the recipe I have used weekly for nearly 30 years now. If, however, you are already a bread-maker and set in your ways don't hesitate to use your own basic bread recipe and add the basil to the milk or water in the recipe.

This is not a heavy, jelly-like crème brulée. Expect it to be a true custard.

This is a good recipe for widgeon or teal or other smaller size ducks.

GRILLED MARINATED DUCKS

- 3 onions
- 4 carrots
- 2 tbsp. unsalted butter
- 1 bottle red wine
- Parsley stems
- Fresh thyme sprigs
- 2 lemon slices
- 1 bay leaf
- 20 crushed peppercorns
- 2 tsp. salt
- 2 ducks, butterflied (see page 255)

Chop the onion and carrots and sauté in the butter till the onions are translucent. Add the red wine and bring to a simmer. Add the remaining ingredients and pour over the ducks. Let marinate for one or two days turning the breasts every so often.

Dry roast the duck in a preheated oven for 20 minutes at 450°.

Grill over a medium-low fire, starting skin side down on the grill for 5 minutes. Turn over and grill 4 more minutes. Take off grill and rest 5 minutes. Cut in portions to serve.

GRILLED RED ONION

2 red onions
2 tbsp. unsalted butter
Salt and pepper

Slice the onions ¼-inch thick and grill or broil them lightly for 2-3 minutes per side. Now sauté them quickly in the butter over a medium heat and season with salt and pepper.

Or you can dribble green olive oil over them and serve hot or cold.

GRILLED MUSHROOMS

1 lb. large mushrooms (whole or halved) like Portobello
3 tbsp. unsalted butter Salt and pepper

Grill or broil the mushrooms for 3-4 minutes and then sauté them in the butter. Season with salt and pepper.

BASIL BREAD

- 2 cups lukewarm to warm water
- 1 tbsp. dry yeast
- 1 tbsp. sugar
- 1 tbsp. salt
- 2 tbsp. dried basil
- 5 cups or so of all-purpose flour (I recommend King Arthur Flour)
- Butter and oil for greasing pans

In the bowl of a standing mix master, fitted with a bread hook, add the warm water and sprinkle in the yeast, sugar, salt, and basil. Let sit for a few minutes until the yeast looks dissolved and foamy. Now pour in 5 cups of flour and mix at the lowest setting, usually marked "stir," until the flour is blended and then increase the speed to the next level, #2. Continue blending at this speed until the dough is well mixed, pulling away from the sides of the bowl, and forming a ball. Turn onto a floured surface and knead the dough for about 8 minutes. It should be slightly tacky to the touch but smooth and very malleable. Place in a bowl that has been oiled, turn the dough over in the oil so the top is oiled, too, and cover the bowl with a cloth. Let rise until it is double in size, about 2 to 3 hours. Punch it down and let it rest while you prepare the pan(s) for it to rise in again.

This recipe makes enough for a baguette and a loaf. I always make a baguette for the week's spaghetti night so I pull a handful of dough off and roll it into a big snake and lay it in one side of a baguette pan that has been buttered. The remaining dough I either place into a buttered loaf pan, pushing it into the rectangle shape, or form a ball with the dough, flouring it heavily, and put into a banneton, also heavily floured. Both the baguette and the loaf/round I cover with a cloth and let rise again for another hour or so.

The breads in the metal baking pans can go directly into a preheated oven at 420° for 35 to 40 minutes until golden brown. The banneton is trickier. I use a piece of parchment paper, floured, atop the back of a cookie sheet and careful invert the banneton and let the dough fall out. Often it loses its rise and I let it sit covered for another hour to rise again. Once the round is ready to bake I slide it onto a pizza stone that is in a preheated oven at 420° and bake it for 40 minutes or until golden. Once baked, I turn the baguette and loaf out of their pans—or slide the round on the parchment onto the cookie sheet—and onto a rack to cool. Let cool for 30 minutes or so before cutting.

If I don't plan to use the baguette that day I wrap it in foil and put it in the freezer to use another day. (It just needs to be taken from the freezer and put in a preheated oven at 350° for 30 minutes or so.)

CRÈME BRULÉE

- 6 eggs
- 5 tbsp. sugar
- 3 cups heavy cream (or 1½ cups heavy cream and 1½ cups whipping cream)
- 1 tbsp. vanilla
- ½–⅔ cup dark brown sugar

Separate the eggs, beat the yolks and combine well with the white sugar and cream. Heat the mixture over a medium heat stirring constantly with a whisk until you can see steam beginning to rise and the custard is starting to form around the edge of the pot. Remove from the burner and add the vanilla. Pour through a strainer into a round, stoneware baking dish that is about 11 inches or so in diameter. Put the dish on a cookie sheet that has sides and surround it with an inch or so of boiling water. Bake it in a preheated oven at 300° for 30 minutes or until the custard is just setting around the edges but is still soft in the middle. Remove from the oven and let it sit in the water-bath while it cools—about 30 minutes. Then refrigerate the custard for at least two hours or overnight. Just before serving sprinkle the custard with the brown sugar and put the dish back on the cookie sheet and this time surround it with ice cubes. Put it under a very hot broiler for a minute or two until the brown sugar burns a bit and forms a nice hard crust. Serve immediately or chill again and serve.

Roasted Duck
Potatoes Steamed with Sage
Bittergreens and Cheese Salad
Tangerine Sorbet

Serves four

A somewhat controversial issue in game cooking is the length of cooking time for ducks. Some people prefer their ducks cooked for 10 or 15 minutes, some for hours. Of course the preference also determines the results. Some like blood red meat, some like leather brown meat. I go with the middle-of-the road system. I prefer to cook our blacks and mallards at 350° for 50 minutes so that they are pink inside but share no risk of being either bloody or leathery. It is, of course, purely a matter of taste not only specifically with ducks but with any meat. If you are uncertain how you prefer your ducks and don't have a large quantity to experiment with, try it my way. This recipe is good for ducks the size of blacks, mallards and pintails.

Be sure to use the liqueur suggested in the sorbet; it makes a difference.

ROASTED DUCK

- 2 carrots
- 1 celery stick
- 2 onions
- 6 parsley stems
- 2 tbsp. bacon fat
- 4 ducks plucked
- 8 sprigs of thyme
- 8 strips of bacon
- 2 cups white wine
- 4 cloves garlic, peeled and crushed
- 1 bay leaf
- Salt and pepper
- 4 tbsp. unsalted butter

Chop the carrots, celery, onion, and parsley stems fine and sauté in fat in the roasting pan. Set ducks on this bed of vegetables. Place 2 sprigs of thyme into the cavity and two strips of bacon on each duck. Add the white wine and bring to a simmer. Now add the garlic, bay leaf, and salt and pepper. Roast in a preheated oven at 350° for 40 minutes, discard the bacon and continue cooking for 10 minutes more to brown them. Remove the ducks and place on a heated platter. Purée the vegetables and juices in the blender, first removing the bay leaf. Strain the purée and return it to the stove whisking in the butter. Season with salt and pepper.

Carve the ducks pouring a little of the sauce over each serving.

POTATOES STEAMED WITH SAGE

- 12 little red potatoes (or what seems the right number for four folks)
- 1 tbsp. crumbled dried sage
- 4 tbsp. unsalted butter
- ¼ cup freshly grated parmesan cheese
- Salt and pepper

Wash and cut the potatoes in half (if they are big). Place the potatoes on a vegetable steaming rack and sprinkle with sage. Put the rack into a saucepan with just a ½ inch of boiling water. Steam covered for 25 minutes or until tender. Put the potatoes into a serving dish and pat with butter. Sprinkle with parmesan cheese and salt and pepper to taste. Toss and serve.

BITTERGREENS AND CHEESE SALAD

      Escarole, chicory and arugula
      Bibb lettuce
      Loaf of French bread
      Garlic clove, sliced in half
5 tbsp. unsalted butter
4 strips of bacon
3 oz. blue cheese
      Vinaigrette
      Salt and pepper

Wash and dry the greens and lettuce and break into bite size pieces. Slice the bread into 1-inch square pieces, rub with garlic, dry in a 300° oven, and then fry in butter. Set aside. Cut the bacon into 1-inch pieces and fry till medium done, not quite crisp. Cut the cheese into small cubes. Combine the lettuce, bacon and cheese and toss with the vinaigrette. Add the croutons and check for seasoning. Serve.

TANGERINE SORBET

15-20 tangerines (enough for 4 cups)
1 cup sugar
      Pinch of salt
      Splash of lemon juice
1 tbsp. Mandarin Napoleon liqueur (tangerine liqueur)
      (Remember to have enough ice and salt for your ice cream freezer, too).

Squeeze enough tangerines so you have 1 quart of juice. Boil ½ a cup of water and add the sugar and cook for 5 minutes. Let cool. Add the sugar syrup to the fruit juice as needed to please your taste. Add the salt and lemon juice to help the taste and then pour in the liqueur. Chill the mixture in the canister from your ice cream maker. Then freeze according to the ice cream machine's directions.

Minted Roast Duck with Potatoes, Carrots and Turnips
Green Salad
Alice Waters' Olive Oil and Sauternes Cake

Serves four

Wild creatures tend to have very little fat. And what fat they do have is not marbled throughout the meat but stored in certain specific locations. It also is fat which, if cooked with the bird, doesn't add much to the taste. Theoretically the fat has all been cleaned out of the bird and in order to cook it so it isn't dried out you must add good-tasting fat or a liquid to the bird while cooking. This recipe suggests a nice technique for doing that and is particularly good for big black ducks.

The olive oil and Sauternes cake doesn't sound very tasty. It is wonderful. It is from Alice Waters' *Chez Panisse Menu Cookbook*.

You know how to make the salad.

MINTED ROAST DUCK WITH POTATOES, CARROTS AND TURNIPS

- ½ cup (1 stick) unsalted butter slightly softened
- 1½ tbsp. dried mint, reconstituted in a little hot water
- Salt, pepper, and a pinch of cayenne
- 2 ducks for roasting
- 4 potatoes
- 4 carrots
- 4 large turnips
- 2 tbsp. bacon fat

Whip the butter. Add the mint, salt, pepper and cayenne to taste and whip again. Carefully pull the skin of the duck slightly away from the meat and slip the butter between the breasts and the skin, covering as much surface as possible.

Peel and quarter the potatoes. Peel the carrots and cut into 2-inch chunks. Peel and halve the turnips. Sauté all three vegetables in the bacon fat. Place the sautéed vegetables in a roasting pan with the ducks and cook at 450° for 10 minutes. Turn the oven down to 325° and finish cooking, about 35 minutes more.

ALICE WATERS' OLIVE OIL AND SAUTERNES CAKE

    5 eggs, plus 2 egg whites
    ¾ cup sugar
    1 tbsp. mixed grated orange and lemon peel
    1 cup sifted flour
    ½ teaspoon salt
    ½ cup good quality Sauternes
    ½ cup plus 2 tbsp. extra virgin olive oil

Preheat the oven to 375°. Separate the 5 eggs and beat the egg yolks with the sugar in a bowl with a whisk attachment for 3 to 5 minutes until light colored and well-beaten. Add the orange and lemon peel and set aside.

Combine sifted flour and salt, then add bit by bit to the sugar-egg mixture, beating continually until it is all incorporated. Add the Sauternes and olive oil in the same fashion.

Beat the 5 egg whites and 2 additional egg whites until they stand in stiff peaks, then stir in ⅓ of the whites. Once well blended, carefully fold the remaining whites into the mixture thoroughly.

Pour this batter into an 8-inch spring-form pan whose bottom has been lined with parchment and whose entire interior has been well buttered and flour dusted. Bake for 20 minutes, rotating the cake if necessary to insure even cooking. After 20 minutes lower the temperature to 325° and bake for another 20 minutes. Then turn off the oven and leave the cake in the closed oven for 10 minutes more while the cake deflates like a fallen soufflé.

Remove the cake from the oven, invert it onto a flat surface, remove from the spring-form pan. Allow it to cool completely.

This cake can be stored, well sealed, in the refrigerator. Serve with fresh peaches and a glass of Sauternes.

Duck Roasted with Red Pepper Butter
Persillade Potatoes
Sautéed Green Beans and Cherry Tomatoes
Almond Cake

Serves four

Sweet roasted red peppers come in little jars from the supermarket. And they are expensive and can be somewhat flavorless. When you roast them yourself they take on a nice charcoal taste and aren't watery from sitting in a jar. Not only are they delicious in the butter as suggested here, but are great in salads. They also can be kept in the refrigerator with a little olive oil for instant salad and sandwich use.

The Sautéed Green Beans and Cherry Tomatoes is something you know how to do. Blanch the beans and prick the tomatoes with a pin before sautéing for best results.

DUCK ROASTED WITH RED PEPPER BUTTER

- ½ cup roasted and peeled red pepper (use about 2-3 red peppers)
- 1 cup (2 sticks) unsalted butter, softened
- 1 garlic clove, chopped fine
- ½ tsp. fresh ground pepper
- Salt
- 4 ducks, butterflied (see page 255)

Preheat the broiler. On a cookie sheet place 2 or 3 red peppers as close as possible to the heat turning them till charred on all sides. Let cool. Once the peppers have cooled remove all charred black skin. Whip the butter till soft and light. Chop the peppers fine and add along with the garlic, pepper, and salt to the butter. Whip together and then let sit in the freezer for several hours. Remove the butter from the freezer an hour or so before serving. Grill the butterflied birds breast side down first for 10 to 15 minutes on high heat, then flip so the bone side is down and reduce the heat. Cook for about 5 to 10 more minutes. Remove and put several slices of compound butter on each duck. Serve.

PERSILLADE POTATOES

½ bunch parsley
2 garlic cloves
2 large potatoes
2 tbsp. bacon fat or butter
Salt and pepper

Chop the parsley and garlic fine and mix together. Peel and slice the potatoes and then sauté them in bacon fat over a medium heat for a few minutes, then with the lid on for five or so minutes. Remove the lid and add the parsley and garlic mixture and cook for several more minutes. Season with salt and pepper and serve.

ALMOND CAKE

¾ cup almonds
6 tbsp. unsalted butter
3 eggs
⅔ cup sugar
½ cup sifted all-purpose flour
3 tbsp. brandy
Dusting of confectioners' sugar

Roast the almonds on a cookie sheet in a 300° oven for about 20 minutes or until they are a nice golden tan. Be sure to shake the almonds often while cooking so they do not get over-done. Chop the almonds very fine. Or this can be done in your food processor.

Melt the butter and when cooled stir in the eggs and sugar. Then add the flour, almonds, and brandy.

Butter and flour an 8-inch square pan and pour the batter into it. Bake at 325° for 20 minutes or until a skewer pulls out clean when you stick it in the center of the cake. Let cool in the pan, then cut into squares and dust with the confectioners' sugar.

Sea Duck Fricassee
Fennel, Mint, Cucumber, Radish Salad
Fried Polenta
Fresh Fruit

Serves four

Duck hunts on the ocean can be marvelous. The only issue being that the most plentiful species of duck there is the sea duck, which are sometimes not the best tasting. The sea ducks that feed on fish and shellfish are a continual challenge to the gourmet cook. How do you prepare them so the fish taste is masked or eliminated but the good game duck taste comes through? In addition to recipes such as these which are heavy on the masking there are a few home techniques of exorcising the fish taste from the duck meat. One such technique which I can vouch for is to breast out the bird and cook the pieces in near-boiling milk for a few minutes and then sauté in butter and serve as an hors d'oeuvre. But for a full main course you might try the following.

SEA DUCK FRICASSEE

- 2 onions, chopped fine
- 1 leek, chopped fine
- 4 carrots, sliced
- 2 cups stock
- 4 ducks, breasted out
- 2 tsp. thyme
- 4 tbsp. unsalted butter
- 2 large tomatoes, skinned, seeded and chopped
- Salt and pepper

Sauté the onions, leeks, and carrots till the onions are translucent. Add the stock and bring to a boil. Let bubble on medium-low heat until the liquid has been reduced by half. Add the duck breasts and thyme and reduce the heat, cover with a piece of foil pressed down to touch the surface of the meat. Simmer over a low heat for 10 minutes or when the breasts feel springy to the touch. Remove the breasts and purée the vegetables with the liquid in a blender or food processor. Return the purée to the heat and reduce it to thicken if necessary. Whisk in the butter and add the tomatoes and duck breasts and heat for a few seconds. Season to taste and serve immediately.

FENNEL, MINT, CUCUMBER, RADISH SALAD

- 1 head fennel
- 2 cucumbers
- 1 bunch radishes
- Several sprigs of mint
- 1 garlic clove
- ¼ cup olive oil
- Salt and pepper

Trim, core, and cut the fennel. Wash and slice the cucumbers and radishes. Chop the mint and garlic finely and add to the vegetables. Pour the olive oil over it all and season with salt and pepper. Toss and serve.

FRIED POLENTA

    1 onion
    ½ cup (1 stick) unsalted butter
    3 cups milk
    1 cup cornmeal
    1 cup water
    ½ tsp. nutmeg
      Salt and pepper
      Fat to fry in (bacon, pancetta or butter)

Chop the onion very fine and sauté it in the butter till translucent. Add the milk and bring it to a boil. Combine the cornmeal and water, stir with a fork, and then add it to the boiling milk and onion mixture. Stir continuously until the mixture is so thick the spoon stands up in it. Remove it from the heat and add the nutmeg and season with salt and pepper. Grease a cookie sheet and spread the polenta ½ to ¼-inch thick on it. Let stand until cool and slightly hardened. Now cut with cookie cutters and fry the shapes in the fat till they are brown. Serve.

Duck with Pancetta and Prosciutto
Roast Potatoes with Rosemary
Fresh Green Peas
Kiwi Ice

Serves four

Fresh green peas are, of course, a springtime item so this menu is intended for that lone duck saved in the freezer from last fall's hunt. Otherwise Birds Eye Tender Tiny Green Peas are okay to use during hunting season.

DUCK WITH PANCETTA AND PROSCIUTTO

- 4 oz. pancetta
- 4 skinned duck breasts, sliced into two flat pieces as if for scaloppini
- 4 slices prosciutto
- 2 tbsp. parsley, chopped fine
- Salt and pepper

Dice the pancetta into ⅛-inch pieces and then sauté till almost crisp. Remove from pan with a slotted spoon and set aside. Sauté the duck breasts in the hot fat and remove when just barely done (remember they'll keep cooking after they've been removed from the pan). Let the breasts cool slightly and slice the pieces on the diagonal. While the duck is cooking, julienne the prosciutto and sauté it quickly for a few minutes. Add the cooked pancetta, duck meat, and parsley and toss. Season with salt and pepper and serve.

ROAST POTATOES WITH ROSEMARY

16 little red potatoes
4 tbsp. melted, unsalted butter or olive oil
   Rosemary
   Salt and pepper

Paint the potatoes with the melted butter and sprinkle liberally with rosemary. Roast in the oven for about 35 minutes at 350° or until they are tender. Season with salt and pepper.

KIWI ICE

24 kiwis (approximately)
½ cup water
1 cup sugar
   Pinch of salt and a few drops of lemon juice
     as needed
1 tbsp. vodka
   (Remember to have enough ice and salt for
     your ice cream freezer, too).

Scoop out the insides of the kiwis and purée in the blender. You should have about 1 quart of purée. Bring the water to a boil and add the sugar and cook for 5 minutes. Let cool. Add the sugar syrup to the fruit juice as needed to please your taste. Add salt and lemon juice to help the taste if need be and then pour in the vodka. Chill the mixture in the canister from your ice cream maker. Then freeze according to the ice cream machine's directions.

Grilled Breast of Duck with Wild Mushrooms and
Honey Mustard Sauce
Soup in a Pumpkin
Olive Oil and Salt Bread
Figs in Rum

Serves four

GRILLED BREAST OF DUCK WITH WILD MUSHROOMS AND HONEY MUSTARD SAUCE

- 4 ducks, breasted out (this recipe can be used for fish-eating ducks)
- 1 shallot, chopped
- ¼ cup olive
- ¾ lb. fresh wild mushrooms (a combination of chanterelles and porcini are my favorite)
- 3 cloves garlic, mashed
- ¼ cup white wine
- 2 tbsp. fresh thyme, chopped
- 2 tbsp. honey mustard
- 1 cup duck demi-glace
- 1 cup heavy cream

Breast out the ducks and let the breast medallions sit while you prepare the sauce. Sauté the shallot in half of the olive oil; add wild mushrooms. When the mushrooms are almost done, add garlic and white wine. Reduce until almost dry. Now add thyme, honey mustard, duck demi-glace and stir until blended. Add heavy cream and turn up the heat bringing the mixture to a boil. Let bubble until thickened and cream mixture is reduced by half. Sauté the duck breasts in the remaining olive oil. Place sautéed mushrooms in center of a hot plate. Slice the duck and arrange around mushrooms.

SOUP IN A PUMPKIN

- 1 perfect little pumpkin which will fit in your oven and weighs about 6 lbs.
- ½ cup (1 stick) unsalted butter
- 1 onion, chopped
- 5 cups chicken stock
  - Bay leaf
  - Several parsley stems
  - Salt and pepper
- ½ cup cream
  - Croutons
  - Chopped parsley

Scoop out the pumpkin. Discard the seeds and string and save the flesh. Be sure not to scoop too close to the skin. Cut the pumpkin flesh into small chunks and sauté it in the butter along with the onion until the pumpkin is soft. Add the stock, bay leaf, and parsley stems. Season with salt and pepper and let cook until the mixture is quite soft. Remove bay leaf. Purée in the blender or a food processor and then strain. Add the cream and check for seasoning. Return the pumpkin soup to the pumpkin shell and cook in the oven for 40 minutes at 350°. Garnish with the croutons and chopped parsley and serve scraping the pumpkin shell sides as you ladle the soup into the bowls.

OLIVE OIL AND SALT BREAD

- 2 cups lukewarm to warm water
- 1 tbsp. dry yeast
- 1 tbsp. sugar
- 1 tbsp. salt
- 2 tbsp. dried thyme
- 5 cups or so of all-purpose flour (I recommend King Arthur Flour)
- ¼ cup good green olive oil
- 1 tbsp. kosher salt
- Butter and oil for greasing pans

In the bowl of a standing mix master, fitted with a bread hook, add the warm water and sprinkle in the yeast, sugar, salt, and thyme. Let sit for a few minutes until the yeast looks dissolved and foamy. Now pour in 5 cups of flour and mix at the lowest setting, usually marked "stir," until the flour is blended and then increase the speed to the next level, #2. Continue blending at this speed until the dough is well mixed, pulling away from the sides of the bowl, and forming a ball. Turn onto a floured surface and knead the dough for about 8 minutes. It should be slightly tacky to the touch but smooth and very malleable. Place in a bowl that has been oiled, turn the dough over in the oil so the top is oiled, too, and cover the bowl with a cloth. Let rise until it is double in size, about 2 to 3 hours. Punch it down and let it rest while you prepare the pan(s) for it to rise in again.

This recipe makes enough for a baguette and a loaf. I always make a baguette for the week's spaghetti night so I pull a handful of dough off and roll it into a big snake and lay it in one side of a baguette pan that has been buttered. The remaining dough I use to make the Olive Oil and Salt bread for this menu by forming a ball with the dough, flouring it heavily, and putting it into a banneton, also heavily floured. Both the baguette and the round I cover with a cloth and let rise again for another hour or so.

Using a banneton can be a bit tricky but it produces a beautiful round of bread. Using a piece of parchment paper, floured, atop the back of a cookie sheet, I carefully invert the banneton and let the dough fall out. I then very carefully poke ¼-inch holes all around the top of the bread with the end of a wooden spoon. Fill the holes with the olive oil (or you can use walnut oil) and sprinkle with the kosher salt Often it loses its rise and I let it sit covered for another hour to rise again. Once the round is ready to bake I slide it onto a pizza stone that is in a preheated oven at 420º and bake it and the baguette for 35 to 40 minutes or until golden. Once baked, I turn the baguette out onto a cooling rack and slide the round on the parchment onto the cookie sheet—also onto the rack to cool. Let cool for 30 minutes or so before cutting.

If I don't plan to use the baguette that day I wrap it in foil and put it in the freezer to use another day. (It just needs to be taken from the freezer and put in a preheated oven at 350º for 30 minutes or so.) .

FIGS IN RUM

2 lbs. fresh figs
1 cup water
1 cup sugar
1 vanilla bean
Pinch of thyme or a sprig of fresh thyme
4 tbsp. rum
1 cup heavy cream

Wash and drain the figs. Simmer the water and sugar together for 5 minutes then add the figs and vanilla bean and thyme. Cook slowly over a low heat for 1 hour. Remove from the heat and let cool. Add the rum and cover the fruit tightly. Let it all sit in the refrigerator for two days. Whip the cream and serve on top of the figs.

Marinated Duck Breasts
Plain Roast Potatoes
Julienned Celery and Zucchini
Strawberry Tart

Serves four

When I first started to hunt and to cook wild game it seemed almost sacrilegious to skin ducks and marinate them. I have since learned that those of us who are fortunate to do a lot of hunting and hunt hard throughout the season don't always end up with the most pristine birds. There are edible ducks that, upon occasion, need some help either because they are badly shot up or have endured a harsh winter. This recipe is for just such a duck.

There are also some ducks which are simply inedible no matter what you do to them. A writer friend of ours, John Hewitt, made his first visit from Alaska to see us in my early hunting days. I knew John to be quite a proficient hunter and outdoorsman. And I assumed that anyone from Alaska must be a subsistence hunter inclined to saving and using everything, from beaks to feet. We sat in our Boston apartment after a long day's hunt, cleaning ducks. John was tasked with plucking the last duck and after several pulls a huge patch of green skin was revealed on the poor little black duck. I was horrified when I saw it, not so much from the sight of it but at the thought that this backwoodsman would probably want to cook and eat it anyway. Pleased I definitely was when I saw John's plucking slow to a stop and the little carcass drop into the garbage can. "We throw those out in Alaska," was all he said. We throw them out here, too. And when in doubt I'd throw any duck out rather than risk the memory of a bad taste or worse.

MARINATED DUCK BREASTS

  8 toasted and crushed juniper berries
10 peppercorns, crushed
  1 tbsp. rosemary
  4 oz. cognac
  4 skinned duck, breasted
  4 oz. pine nuts
  3 tbsp. unsalted butter

Combine the juniper berries, peppercorns, rosemary and cognac in a bowl and place the skinned breasts in it to marinate 24 hours. Be sure to turn them in the marinade every so often.

Sauté the pine nuts in a tablespoon of the butter until light brown and remove from the pan. Now add the remaining two tablespoons of butter and sauté the duck until done. Serve with the pine nuts sprinkled on top.

JULIENNED CELERY AND ZUCCHINI

6 stalks celery
1 zucchini
2 tbsp. unsalted butter
   Salt and pepper

Scrape the outside of each celery stalk (except for the young tender ones) with a vegetable peeler and cut into 2-inch lengths. Now julienne into ⅛-inch sticks. Cut the zucchini skin off in thick strips, discard the interior part of the zucchini and then julienne the skin into ⅛-inch sticks. Sauté the celery and zucchini together in butter till they are hot but still crisp. Season with salt and pepper.

STRAWBERRY TART

- 1 sheet Pepperidge Farm Puff Pastry or your own (or mine, p.250)
- 1 tbsp. butter for buttering dish
- 2 tbsp. sugar for sprinkling on pastry
- ½ pint heavy cream
- ½ tbsp. Grand Marnier (or your choice of liqueur)
- 3 tbsp. sour cream
- 2 pints strawberries
- 2 tbsp. currant jam

Preheat the oven at 425° for at least 20 minutes.

Roll out the pastry and fit into a porcelain tart or quiche dish heavily buttered. Roll the rolling pin over the top to cut the extra pastry off the edges. Let rest in the refrigerator for 1 hour. Prick the pastry with a fork and then flatten a piece of foil over it. Put beans, peas, or pastry weights on top of the foil. Cook in the lower part of the hot oven for 7 minutes, then carefully open the oven and remove the foil and weights. Sprinkle with sugar and continue cooking for at least 5 minutes until the crust is a light brown with a shiny, caramelized surface. Then remove from the oven and let cool 1 minute. Slide the pastry out of the dish onto a cake rack to cool completely. Whip the cream. About half way through whipping add the Grand Marnier (Framboise is good, too) and the sour cream. Spread over the bottom of the pastry shell. Arrange the strawberries on top of the cream attractively (raspberries, blueberries or any fruit are good also). Melt the currant jam over a low flame. Remove and let cool slightly. To the jam add a dash of the liqueur you used in the cream. Now, with a 2-inch pastry brush, paint the strawberries with the jam mixture. Serve immediately as it will become soggy if you try to hold it more than one hour.

Grilled Lemon Duck
Grated Zucchini
Sautéed Cherry Tomatoes
Grilled Bread
Pear Cake

Serves four

The ducks in this recipe must be butterflied. This is not some unusual bird/animal act but rather a method of preparing the duck so it will cook completely evenly. By flattening the bird out to bake it is less likely to dry out in the legs and breast. Butterflying can be done to any duck (and upland birds, too) but is particularly good for the smaller ducks. Teal are suggested for this recipe.

GRILLED LEMON DUCK

- 1 sweet red onion
- 4 ducks, butterflied
- Salt and pepper
- Oregano
- 6 lemons, sliced very thin
- Olive oil

Peel and slice the onion and lay it on the bottom of a large roasting pan. Butterfly (see page 255) and flatten the breasts of the ducks and season with salt, pepper and oregano. Set the breasts skin side up on top of the onions and completely cover with the lemon slices. Paint with olive oil, cover and refrigerate overnight.

One hour before cooking remove the ducks from the refrigerator. Take the lemon slices off and reserve (also reserve the onion slices). Baste the duck again with the oil. Grill the breasts, bone side first, quickly on both sides and return to the onions. Replace the lemon slices and baste again with olive oil. Roast at 350° for 35 minutes. (Make any necessary adjustments for time and temperature depending on size of the bird). Season with salt and pepper.

GRATED ZUCCHINI

- 4 medium zucchini
- Salt
- 1 lb. spinach
- 1 shallot, chopped
- 2 tbsp. unsalted butter
- Salt and pepper

Grate the zucchini coarsely. Put it in a strainer and sprinkle with salt. Let stand and drain for 20 minutes. Meanwhile wash the spinach, shake dry, and barely wilt it over a medium-low flame with the lid on for a second. Drain the spinach, let cool, then chop. Squeeze the water out of the zucchini. Sauté the shallot in butter over a medium heat and add the zucchini to it. Add the spinach. Stirring continuously, heat the vegetables over medium heat till hot to the touch. Add salt and pepper to taste and serve.

SAUTÉED CHERRY TOMATOES

- 24 cherry tomatoes
- 2 tbsp. unsalted butter
- Several sprigs of fresh basil (or any other fresh herb you may have; dried herbs work, too)
- Salt and pepper

Prick each cherry tomato with a pin to prevent the tomato skins from bursting and remove the green tops. Sauté in the butter till hot and sprinkle with the chopped herb and salt and pepper. Serve.

GRILLED BREAD

1 loaf of French bread
1 garlic clove cut in half
About ½ cup good green olive oil

Slice the bread into ½-inch pieces and rub each side with the garlic. Grill over a medium-low fire and then pour a little of the olive oil on each piece.

PEAR CAKE

2 eggs
¼ cup milk
2 tsp. vanilla, pear liqueur or rum
1 cup sugar
Pinch of salt
Rind of one orange, grated
1½ cups flour
2 lbs. fresh pears
Butter to grease the cake pan
½ cup unflavored bread crumbs

Preheat the oven to 350°. Beat the eggs, milk and vanilla (or liqueur) together in a bowl. Add the sugar, salt and orange rind and continue beating. Now blend in the flour. Peel the pears and cut them in half. Scoop out the seeds and core and slice into pieces no more than 1 inch thick and add to the flour, egg, and sugar mixture. Grease a 9-inch cake pan with butter and then sprinkle finely-ground bread crumbs into it. Shake the crumbs all about and then empty the pan of any excess crumbs. Pour the batter into the cake tin and level it with a spoon. Bake in the preheated oven for 45 minutes or until it is a light brown. Let it cool and then remove it from the pan. The pear cake can be eaten lukewarm or cold. It's good served with a lightly whipped cream, too.

Smoked Goose Salad
Butternut Squash Soup
Sun-dried Tomato Bread
Chocolate Cake

Serves four

The next two menus involve using smoked goose. I like to smoke our geese because I never really found a method of roasting which made them taste as romantic as the recipe made them sound. Geese are big, tough birds in general and even though they are terrific fun to shoot, I'd rather eat a black duck any day. So the smoking helps considerably. There are, of course, several types of smoking methods and many types of smokers. We use a hot smoke technique and a charcoal cooker. The charcoal cookers are a little bit more difficult to control than electric ones but definitely produce the desired results. I suggest following the manufacturer's directions on how to rig the cooker. Use a piece of green, fruit-tree wood on the coals; this will affect the taste. Use beer or wine in the water. It appears to have absolutely no effect on the taste but esthetically is much more pleasing. Do not smoke the goose for as long as is recommended. We usually do our geese for only an hour even though much more is recommended. The length of time is greatly affected by the outside temperature where the smoker sits. Just remember that it is always possible to cook something more, but impossible to un-cook an over-done bird.

SMOKED GOOSE SALAD

- 1 smoked goose
- Rind from 1 orange
- 4 celery stalks
- 1 apple
- ½ cup walnuts, toasted and chopped fine
- ½ cup walnut oil
- 1 tsp. shallots, chopped fine
- 1 tbsp. vinegar
- 1 tsp. prepared mustard
- 1 tsp. tarragon
- Salt and pepper
- Lettuce leaves (Boston or Bibb or any type that would make a nice bed of lettuce)

Remove the smoked meat from the bones of the goose. The skin of a smoked goose is worth saving as it contains much of the flavor so leave it on the meat. Cut the meat into bite-size pieces and set aside. Peel the orange making sure not to get any of the white pith. Blanch and julienne the peel. Set aside. Peel the celery stalks and apple and cut into nice size pieces. Toast the walnuts. Combine the goose, orange rind, apple, celery and walnuts. Make a vinaigrette in the blender with the remaining ingredients and pour over the goose mixture and toss. Check for seasoning and serve on a bed of lettuce.

BUTTERNUT SQUASH SOUP

1 butternut squash
¾ cup unsalted butter
1 tbsp. thyme
1 tsp. nutmeg
2 cups chicken stock
1 cup heavy cream
  Salt and pepper

Peel the squash so there is no beige, hard skin on it. Remove the seeds and any of the stringy darker insides with a spoon. Cube and sauté the squash in ½ cup of butter over a medium-low heat until the squash is very soft. Purée the squash in a blender or food processor and strain it back into the sauté pan. Add the remaining ¼ cup butter, thyme, nutmeg, and stock and cook gently, stirring with a wire whisk, until all ingredients are well combined and hot. Add the cream and stir for another minute or two. Check for salt and pepper and serve.

SUN-DRIED TOMATO BREAD

2 cups lukewarm to warm water
1 tbsp. dry yeast
1 tbsp. sugar
1 tbsp. salt
5 cups all-purpose flour
½ cup sun-dried tomatoes
¼ cup olive oil
  Sprig of thyme
¼ cup wine
⅓ cup pitted black olives, chopped coarsely
  Butter or oil for greasing pans

In the bowl of a standing mix master, fitted with a bread hook, add the warm water and sprinkle in the yeast, sugar, and salt. Let sit for a few minutes until the yeast looks dissolved and foamy. Now pour in 5 cups of flour and mix at the lowest setting, usually marked "stir," until the flour is blended and then increase the speed to the next level, #2. Continue blending at this speed until the dough is well mixed, pulling away from the sides of the bowl, and forming a ball. Reconstitute the tomatoes by cooking them in the oil, thyme, and wine over a medium-low heat until they are soft. Let them cool and then chop them coarsely. Add both the olive and the reconstituted tomatoes to the dough. Turn onto a floured surface and knead the dough for about 8 minutes. It should be slightly tacky to the touch but smooth and very malleable. Place in a bowl that has been oiled, turn the dough over in the oil so the top is oiled, too, and cover the bowl with a cloth. Let rise until it is double in size, about 2 to 3 hours. Punch it down and let it rest while you prepare the pan(s) for it to rise in again.

This recipe makes enough for a baguette and a loaf. I always make a baguette for the week's spaghetti night so I pull a handful of dough off and roll it into a big snake and lay it in one side of a baguette pan that has been buttered. The remaining dough I use to make the Sun-dried Tomato bread for this menu by forming a ball with the dough, flouring it heavily, and putting it into a banneton, also heavily floured. Both the baguette and the round I cover with a cloth and let rise again for another hour or so.

Using a banneton can be a bit tricky but it produces a beautiful round of bread. Using a piece of parchment paper, floured, atop the back of a cookie sheet, I carefully invert the banneton and let the dough fall out. Often it loses its rise and I let it sit covered for another hour to rise again. Once the round is ready to bake I slide it onto a pizza stone that is in a preheated oven at 420º and bake it and the baguette for 35 to 40 minutes or until golden. Once baked, I turn the baguette out onto a cooling rack and slide the round on the parchment onto the cookie sheet—also onto the rack to cool. Let cool for 30 minutes or so before cutting.

If I don't plan to use the baguette that day I wrap it in foil and put it in the freezer to use another day. (It just needs to be taken from the freezer and put in a preheated oven at 350º for 30 minutes or so.) .

CHOCOLATE CAKE

- ½ lb. (2 sticks) unsalted butter
- ½ lb. unsweetened chocolate (the better the chocolate, the better the cake)
- 1 tbsp. lemon juice
- 2 tbsp. orange liqueur (Cointreau)
- 1 tbsp. vanilla
- 10 eggs, separated
- 1½ cups sugar
- Pinch of salt
- Sprinkle of confectioners' sugar

Butter and flour a 10-inch spring form pan. Cut a 10-inch round of parchment paper and butter and flour that, placing it on the bottom of the spring form pan.

Combine the butter and chocolate in a saucepan and melt both over a low flame. Stir in the lemon juice, liqueur and vanilla. Remove from the heat. Separate the eggs and beat together the egg yolks and sugar until they ribbon lightly and then combine with the chocolate mixture. Beat the egg whites until they just support a whole raw egg without sinking, but are not too stiff. Then stir in ⅓ of the whites into the chocolate mixture. Fold in the remaining whites.

Pour the cake batter into the pan and bake in a preheated oven of 250° for 2½ hours. Turn off the oven and leave the cake in there for 30 minutes. Remove from the oven and let cool completely. Slide a knife around the cake pan, invert on a plate, and release the spring form pan. Remove the paper carefully and sprinkle with confectioners' sugar.

Smoked Goose in Cold Pasta Salad
Pepperoni Bread
Almond Cake

Serves four

The goose and pasta salad in this menu requires the use of grapes. Grapes, generally speaking, should be peeled if they are to be used in a cold salad. However, you will notice I have not said that here. I envision this menu for a Sunday supper with one's spouse and favorite friends and where a modest amount of effort over the meal is desirable. Peeling grapes for a meal like this seems silly. If, however, the Queen of England is coming for lunch it is advisable to peel the grapes as they will blend better in the salad.

SMOKED GOOSE IN COLD PASTA SALAD

- 1 smoked goose
- ½ cup hazelnut oil
- 2 tbsp. red wine
- 3 tbsp. cream
- 1 tsp. prepared mustard
- Salt and pepper
- ½ lb. pasta
- ½ cup red, seedless grapes cut in half
- ½ cup green, seedless grapes cut in half

Remove the smoked meat from the bones of the goose. The skin of a smoked goose is good and can be left with the meat. Cut the meat into bite-size pieces and set aside. Combine all the remaining ingredients—but for the pasta and grapes—in the blender to make a vinaigrette. Cook the pasta al dente and let cool but not become cold. Toss the pasta, goose, grapes and vinaigrette together and check for seasoning.

PEPPERONI BREAD

- 2 cups lukewarm to warm water
- 1 tbsp. dry yeast
- 1 tbsp. sugar
- 1 tbsp. salt
- 5 cups all-purpose flour
- ⅔ cup pepperoni, chopped
- Butter or oil for greasing pans

In the bowl of a standing mix master, fitted with a bread hook, add the warm water and sprinkle in the yeast, sugar, and salt. Let sit for a few minutes until the yeast looks dissolved and foamy. Now pour in 5 cups of flour and mix at the lowest setting, usually marked "stir," until the flour is blended and then increase the speed to the next level, #2. Continue blending at this speed until the dough is well mixed, pulling away from the sides of the bowl, and forming a ball. Add the chopped pepperoni to the dough. Turn onto a floured surface and knead the dough for about 8 minutes. It should be slightly tacky to the touch but smooth and very malleable. Place in a bowl that has been oiled, turn the dough over in the oil so the top is oiled, too, and cover the bowl with a cloth. Let rise until it is double in size, about 2 to 3 hours. Punch it down and let it rest while you prepare the pan(s) for it to rise in again.

This recipe makes enough for a baguette and a loaf. I always make a baguette for the week's spaghetti night so I pull a handful of dough off and roll it into a big snake and lay it in one side of a baguette pan that has been buttered. The remaining dough I use to make the Pepperoni bread for this menu by forming a ball with the dough, flouring it heavily, and putting it into a banneton, also heavily floured. Both the baguette and the round I cover with a cloth and let rise again for another hour or so.

Using a banneton can be a bit tricky but it produces a beautiful round of bread. Using a piece of parchment paper, floured, atop the back of a cookie sheet, I carefully invert the banneton and let the dough fall out. Often it loses its rise and I let it sit covered for another hour to rise again. Once the round is ready to bake I slide it onto a pizza stone that is in a preheated oven at 420º and bake it and the baguette for 35 to 40 minutes or until golden. Once baked, I turn the baguette out onto a cooling rack and slide the round on the parchment onto the cookie sheet—and also onto the rack to cool. Let cool for 30 minutes or so before cutting.

If I don't plan to use the baguette that day I wrap it in foil and put it in the freezer to use another day. (It just needs to be taken from the freezer and put in a preheated oven at 350º for 30 minutes or so.) .

ALMOND CAKE

- ¾ cup almonds
- 6 tbsp. unsalted butter
- ⅔ cup sugar
- 3 eggs
- ½ cup sifted all-purpose flour
- 3 tbsp. brandy
- Dusting of confectioners' sugar

Roast the almonds on a cookie sheet in a 300° oven for about 20 minutes or until they are a nice golden tan. Be sure to shake the almonds often while cooking so they do not get over-done. Chop the almonds very fine. This can be done in a food processor if you like.

Melt the butter and when cooled stir in the sugar and eggs. Then add the flour, almonds and brandy.

Butter and flour an 8-inch square pan and pour the batter into it. Bake at 325° for 20 minutes or until a skewer pulls out clean when you stick it in the center of the cake. Let cool in the pan, then cut into squares and dust with the confectioners' sugar.

Christmas Goose Anytime
Pignolis and Raisin Cognac Stuffing
Sautéed Mustard Greens
Cooked Apples
Cornsticks
Good Floating Island

Serves four

Despite the fact my taste buds prefer smoked goose, my mind and heart belong to Dickens. Nothing sounds better than a roast goose. Maybe it's because I expect so much that I've been disappointed but also because so many recipes for goose have clearly never been designed for a wild goose. Wild geese are fatless and dry out easily when cooked if they are not basted and stuffed with other types of fat. They do not need to be cooked for hours; quite the contrary. Also, the cavity of the bird must be meticulously cleaned if you plan to use a stuffing (which is desirable to aid in keeping the meat moist) as blood will not enhance the taste of any stuffing I know about. (I have suggested making more than enough stuffing in this recipe so some can be cooked outside of the bird.) Also, I'd suggest not shooting at the lead bird in the vee as it is the toughest and oldest of all the birds and will not taste as good. (As I write this I smile. I'd like to meet the enthusiastic hunter who can resist and be patient enough to not take aim at the lead goose.) Hope for a shot at a lone goose and then try this very nice recipe.

CHRISTMAS GOOSE ANYTIME

1 Canada goose (about 6 or 7 lbs. dressed)

Stuffing ingredients:
- 1 cup onion, chopped fine
- 1 small celery stick, chopped fine
- 1 lb. sweet Italian sausage, chopped
- 1½ tsp. fennel seeds
- ½ cup (1 stick) unsalted butter; plus 1 additional stick of butter to soak cheese cloth in for covering the goose
- ¼ cup cognac

¼ cup golden raisins, soaked in hot cognac
5 tbsp. pignolis nuts, toasted
1½ cup raw rice, cooked
¼ cup chopped parsley
¼ tsp. dried thyme
Salt and pepper
1 egg

To make the stuffing sauté the onion, celery, sausage and fennel seeds together in the butter till everything looks a light brown. Meanwhile soak the raisins in the hot cognac for 15 minutes and then combine both with nuts, rice, parsley, thyme and toss with salt and pepper. Let cool. Beat the egg and mix into the stuffing. Pack ½ of the stuffing or so into the cavity of the bird and truss tightly. Melt the remaining stick of butter. Rinse enough cheese cloth to cover the bird in water and wringing it out, then soak it in the melted butter and spread it over the goose. Roast at 350° for about an hour or 10 minutes per pound, basting frequently.

Place the other half of the stuffing mixture in a baking dish and cook in the same oven with the goose for the last ½ hour of the bird's roasting.

SAUTÉED MUSTARD GREENS

1 bunch mustard greens
2 strips of bacon
Salt and pepper

Remove any of the large stems (larger than a pencil) from the mustard greens and wash the greens. Fry the bacon until almost crisp and remove from the pan. Add the mustard greens to the frying pan with the bacon fat still in it and cook quickly with the lid on for a few minutes till wilted. Chop up the bacon and add it to the greens. Season with salt and pepper.

COOKED APPLES

    3 tbsp. unsalted butter
    4 apples
    1 tbsp. calvados
    ¼ cup cream
      Salt and pepper

Make noisette butter by melting the butter over a medium-high heat in a frying pan until the butter has turned a light brown (remember it continues to darken after it is taken from the heat). Meanwhile peel and dice the apples. Cook them in the butter until just tender on a medium heat. Turn the heat to high, add the calvados and let the heat evaporate it. Pour in the cream and cook a few minutes until the cream has thickened. Season with salt and pepper.

CORNSTICKS

    1½ cups cornmeal
    2 tsp. baking powder
    1 tsp. salt
    ¼ cup flour
    2 tbsp. sugar
    2 eggs
    1 cup buttermilk
    3 tbsp. bacon drippings

Sift together the cornmeal, baking powder, salt, flour and sugar. Beat the eggs, then add the buttermilk and bacon drippings and combine with the dry ingredients. Bake in a 425° oven for 15 to 25 minutes (depends on whether you cook them in cornstick molds or muffin tins).

GOOD FLOATING ISLAND

For the custard:
- 12 eggs, separated
- ¼ tsp. salt
- 1 cup sugar
- 3 cups medium cream
- 2 tbsp. vanilla or liqueur (Grand Marnier, Tia Maria or rum are good)

For the islands:
- 12 egg whites
- Pinch of salt
- ½ cup sugar

For the caramel sauce:
- ⅔ cup sugar
- ¼ cup water

To make the custard, whisk together the egg yolks, ¼ teaspoon salt and 1 cup of the sugar until they are just combined. Add the cream and mix well trying not to make any foam. Pour into a heavy-bottomed saucepan and heat over a medium flame. Stir constantly as it will get hot slowly and then thicken quite suddenly. Watch carefully, and as soon you see steam rising from the pot and the custard thickening remove from the heat and pour through a strainer. Whisk till cool. Add the vanilla or liqueur and refrigerate at least an hour. (The custard may be made the day before.)

To make the islands beat the egg whites, with the pinch of salt, until soft peaks are formed. Then add ½ cup sugar and beat until the whites are smooth and stiff.

Now make caramel sauce by putting ⅔ cup sugar and ¼ cup water into a frying pan and cooking over a high heat until it foams and bubbles and becomes a golden caramel. Remove immediately from the heat and use as it will continue to darken and become stiff. If it becomes too hard add a little water and warm over a low heat.

Smooth the custard into a low serving dish and spoon the whites on top in blobs to form the islands. Take a fork and dip it into the caramelized sugar. Crisscross the islands of whites with the caramelized fork, dipping it every time a criss or cross is made.

This dessert can sit finished for about an hour if the egg whites have been beaten enough.

Mixed Bag

For more years than I care to admit, I was afraid to go hunting by myself. Without Ed to direct me around the marsh in the dark, or handle the dog, I was convinced I was incapable of survival afield. But as the impracticality of always hunting together (who can find a babysitter other than a husband at 4:30 in the morning) became more apparent, I knew I must learn to venture out alone.

My hunting attire laid out the night before to prevent darkroom fumble, I was releasing the dog from his pen not more than ten minutes after the alarm had gone off. With six confirming pats to my breast pocket for my license, another reexamination of the shells in each side pocket (duck loads in the right side, goose loads in the left), I was happy I had not spent the time to stop for coffee—I certainly didn't need the extra buzz. There was a half-hour's drive to the marsh and then a ten-minute marsh walk for this morning pass shoot at black ducks. There sure seemed to be more ditches in the marsh to cross than I remembered and it did seem unusually dark. I realized that I'd forgotten to borrow Ed's watch with the little light in it so I would know when the legal shooting time had arrived. I'd have to estimate the length of time that had transpired from my last glance at the car clock. I could do that, couldn't I? (What a Doubting Dolly I was becoming). I waited in my spot and heard the whistle of wings and saw the speeding dots pass before me. It must be time now. The dog was quivering next to me. I saw the perfect shot coming. I fired and the duck tumbled and bounced on the ground—across the big creek. I sent the dog. But the dog was not trained to do his fancy retrieves—like across the big creek—for me, only for Ed. I had to send the dog again and again. When he finally made it to the other side of the creek he couldn't find the duck. And then I began to doubt where I thought it had fallen, and then to doubt that I'd even seen it fall. Maybe I'd shot at an illegal time? It was dark and with those high expectations my eyes played funny, anticipatory tricks. What made matters worse is that I had spent so much time trying to get the dog to do the retrieving that I'd allowed the tide to come up in the creek to the point of being totally un-crossable in my hip-boots. Now I had to go find a boat. I spent the next hour or so borrowing a friend's boat, paddling to the other side of the creek and scouting for my duck. It would have been so nice if my first time out alone I had come back with dinner. But it was not to be. The friend who lent me the boat did tell me sometime later that their dog had found a half disintegrated duck in that part of the marsh several days later. Maybe it was mine.

I was disappointed in the lack of success in my first solo hunt, but happy to have moved closer to self-reliance afield and to have addressed a real challenge. I had literally lived on that marsh and hunted it for three years with Ed before doing it myself. Nothing could have been more mechanical. But of course nothing interesting in life is truly mechanical. The duck will fall in a difficult location to reach; the dog will balk at the hand-signals; the phone will ring in the middle of rolling out the pastry dough; the child will demand attention when the venison is ready to serve. Instruction, repetition and practice have only made it all as good as it can be. Just as a hunt can't be routine, these recipes cannot guarantee that you will reach the total Nirvana of perfectly executed game dinners without still having some moments of doubt and disappointment.

I've tried to present good guidelines and not be definitive in this book, in order to encourage flexibility, a sense of adventure, experimentation and independence in your game cooking. There are no absolutes, especially in game cooking, which is why it is challenging—and really fun to do.

I always try to write about what I know. And here I've resisted being comprehensive in exchange, hopefully, for providing a reliable base of knowledge for cooking game—leaving out that kangaroo recipe since I've never hunted, cooked or eaten 'roo. Tempting as it is to try and sound smart about all game cooking, I readily admit I don't know how to cook every type of game—any more than I know how to hunt ever type of game—and thus this chapter is thin by comparison to the "Upland Birds," "Water Fowl" and "Venison" chapters. And although I have cooked everything in this chapter at least once, this was the game I was less practiced with or bound by my own, or others, set ways. And like hunting ducks solo, I had to be more independent and improvise when problems arose. I also had a lot of fun with concocting these recipes and menus.

Roast Leg of Mountain Goat
Blue Cheese Polenta
Mixed Green Salad
Alice Waters' Olive Oil and Sauternes Cake

Serves four

ROAST LEG OF MOUNTAIN GOAT

- 1 leg of goat
- 2 garlic cloves
- 2 tbsp. rosemary
- ¼ cup oil
- ½ cup (1 stick) unsalted butter
- Salt and pepper

Clean off all fat from the leg with a little knife. Peel and sliver one of the cloves of garlic. Insert, at a slight angle, the slivers of garlic and ¼ teaspoon of the rosemary. Then rub it all with the oil and the rest of the rosemary and let stand in the refrigerator overnight wrapped in foil. Bring to room temperature before roasting. Preheat the oven to 400° and roast for 30 minutes (or about 10 minutes per pound). Then let sit for 15 minutes or so before carving. An hour or even a day before cooking the goat, make a compound butter by whipping together the butter, the last garlic clove chopped fine, and the remaining teaspoon of rosemary, also chopped fine. Salt and pepper to taste. Wrap in plastic wrap and shape into a log, place in the refrigerator. When the leg is ready sprinkle with salt and pepper and serve with the compound butter.

BLUE CHEESE POLENTA

- 1 small onion (optional)
- 6 tbsp. unsalted butter
- 2 cups milk
- ¾ cup cornmeal
- 5 oz. blue cheese, diced
- ½ tsp. nutmeg
- 2 tsp. kosher salt
- ½ cup heavy cream
- Pepper

If you are using the onion, sauté it in 2 tablespoons of the butter until translucent. Then, in a small saucepan bring the onion, remaining butter, and milk to a boil. Add the cornmeal slowly, stirring constantly till thick and the spoon can stand up in it. Be careful as the polenta will spit at you. Now add the cheese, nutmeg and salt. Remove from the heat and beat in the cream and pepper. Turn immediately into buttered muffin tins and let rest till set. Remove from the tin and put in a heavy oven-proof pan and cook at 400° for 15 minutes (if you like, you can add a little more cheese to the tops of the polenta muffins before putting them in the oven.)

ALICE WATERS' OLIVE OIL AND SAUTERNES CAKE

- 5 eggs, plus 2 egg whites
- ¾ cup sugar
- 1 tbsp. mixed grated orange and lemon peel
- 1 cup sifted flour
- ½ teaspoon salt
- ½ cup good quality Sauternes
- ½ cup plus 2 tbsp. extra virgin olive oil

Preheat the oven to 375°. Separate the 5 eggs and beat the egg yolks with the sugar in a bowl with a whisk attachment for 3 to 5 minutes until light colored and well-beaten. Add the orange and lemon peel and set aside.

Combine sifted flour and salt, then add bit by bit to the sugar-egg mixture, beating continually until it is all incorporated. Add the Sauternes and olive oil in the same fashion.

Beat the 5 egg whites and 2 additional egg whites until they stand in stiff peaks, then stir in ⅓ of the whites. Once well blended, carefully fold the remaining whites into the mixture thoroughly.

Pour this batter into an 8-inch spring-form pan whose bottom has been lined with parchment and whose entire interior has been well buttered and flour dusted. Bake for 20 minutes, rotating the cake if necessary to insure even cooking. After 20 minutes lower the temperature to 325° and bake for another 20 minutes. Then turn off the oven and leave the cake in the closed oven for 10 minutes more while the cake deflates like a fallen soufflé.

Remove the cake from the oven, invert it onto a flat surface, remove from the spring-form pan. Allow it to cool completely. This cake can be stored, well sealed, in the refrigerator. Serve with fresh peaches and a glass of Sauternes.

Braised Bear
Baby Artichokes
Fava Beans, Peas, and Pancetta
Fresh Fruit

Serves four

I have never actually hunted bear although I have cooked it several times and been in camp with spring bear hunters (we were fishing). We had a bear carcass near our duck camp in Alaska (the local Indians had taken the edible meat and left the rest). And we once came upon some bear hunters while we were hunting partridge.

The bear hunters were tracking with dogs and had an eery resemblance to the folks they hired to do the movie "Deliverance." The dead carcass near our duck camp proved an inconvenience. The two retrievers with us loved to roll in it and then cuddled up at night near us for warmth from the Alaskan fall air. Our bear hunting friends, camping near us while we were landlocked salmon fishing, caused only the greatest of amusement. Left early one morning to huddle over bait (garbage) in hopes of attracting a bear, their guide and only means of getting out of the woods went off ... to get drunk. As darkness fell, the hung-over guide tried desperately to remember where he had parked his "sports." The night passed and so did many hours of aimless 3-wheeler driving through a lot of the Maine backwoods. The bear hunters were eventually found with black fly bites as big as baseballs and stories of the thrill of sitting over garbage while the springtime sun heated up—and then went ominously down. A little bleary-eyed, but amazingly cheerful, I remember wondering what the appeal was for those bear hunters. Certainly my brief encounters with bear hunting have left me with no great desire to do it.

My bear-*cooking* experiences have, however, been slightly more persuasive—conjuring great images of the lumbering creatures lurking through the wonderful woods of Maine or Michigan or Alaska. The meat must be cooked long (for fear of any possible trichinosis) and therefore is cooked with many herbs, spices and, in this case, much garlic. It is very aromatic and wonderful for the pre-meal anticipation. Of all the recipes that I submitted when I was the expert editor for the 75th anniversary addition of the *Joy of Cooking*, bear was the favorite of those New York, test kitchen types—it was especially good quality bear meat I supplied them with also, not always the case with bear.

This menu is designed for spring bear as it is the only time fava beans or the baby artichokes are available. Also, don't let the amount of garlic scare you. After it cooks for so long it takes on a very mild and sweet flavor.

BRAISED BEAR

- 8 lbs. bear meat cut into 2-inch cubes
- ½ cup corn oil
- 1 cup onion
- 3 peeled carrots
- 1 large stalk of celery
- 1½ sticks of unsalted butter
- 1 bottle of good red Rhône wine
- 2 cups veal or chicken stock
- 40 garlic cloves,
- 2 tsp. thyme
- 1 bay leaf
- A few parsley stems
- Salt and pepper

Brown the meat in the corn oil and set aside. Discard the oil. Chop the onion, carrot and celery and sauté in the same pan as the bear with 2 tablespoons of butter. Add the browned bear meat to the vegetables and pour in the wine and stock. Bring it to a boil and then reduce to a simmer. Add the garlic cloves, thyme, bay leaf, and parsley stems to the meat mixture. Cover the pan with foil, pressing down so there is no space between the liquid and the foil and the foil is tight over the sides of the pan. Now cover with the lid and continue simmering until done, about 2-3 hours or when a skewer comes out of a piece of meat easily. Skim off any fat. Remove the meat and discard the bay leaf. Strain the liquid and purée both the liquid and the vegetables in a blender in batches if necessary. Return the mixture to the stove and reduce over a medium heat by ⅓ the quantity. Whisk in the remaining butter and check for salt and pepper. Return the meat to the sauce and reheat for a few minutes. Serve.

BABY ARTICHOKES

- 8-10 baby artichokes (the very small artichokes that are about 2 inches long and which will have

no choke)
Juice from 1 lemon (3 tbsp.)
2 tbsp. parsley
1 garlic clove
3 tbsp. olive oil
1 bay leaf
½ tsp. thyme
Salt and pepper
3-4 cups chicken stock
Butter

Remove the outer leaves of the artichoke. Trim the top and bottoms and cut each artichoke lengthwise into slices about ¼-inch thick. Keep them in a lemon and water bath while preparing. Chop the parsley and garlic very fine and sauté in olive oil. Add the artichokes, bay leaf, and thyme. Salt and pepper to taste and toss. Pour in the chicken broth so that the chokes are half covered. Simmer with the lid on for 20 minutes turning the artichokes every now and then. Remove the lid and turn up the heat. Stir until the liquid has almost evaporated. Test for seasoning. Place the artichokes on a serving platter and dot with butter. Serve.

FAVA BEANS, PEAS, AND PANCETTA

1 lb. fava beans
4 oz. pancetta
2 lbs. fresh peas or 1 box frozen peas, defrosted
(Birds Eye Tender Tiny Peas are best)
Salt and pepper
Butter (optional)

Remove the fava beans from their pods. Peel the outer skin from each bean. This is very tedious and boring but important and worth doing. Steam the beans till barely done, about 5 to 10 minutes and cool in ice water, then drain. Dice the pancetta into ⅛-inch pieces and sauté over a low heat until it is not quite crispy. Remove it from the pan. Blanch the fresh peas. Put the peas and the fava beans into the pan where the pancetta was and, over a medium flame, heat through. Put into a serving dish, add salt, pepper and pancetta and a little butter and toss.

Boar Chops with Pernod and Mustard Butter
Gaufrette Potatoes
Fiddleheads
Raspberry Tart

Serves four

This menu suggests gaufrette potatoes which requires the use of a mandoline. This is a piece of equipment which has an outrageous price tag but is very chic—and useful. Since what I am really suggesting for this menu are more commonly known as homemade French fries or "chips," you can save the mandoline for when the Queen comes to lunch.

To make the fries you simply slice the potatoes and deep-fat fry them. But may I also suggest: Leaving the skin on for a stronger potato flavor, using fresh peanut oil each time (re-use the oil only in desperation) and keep the done fries in the oven while the remainder cook.)

BOAR CHOPS WITH PERNOD AND MUSTARD BUTTER

- 1½ sticks unsalted butter, slightly softened
- 1 tbsp. good prepared mustard
- 3 tbsp. Pernod
- Salt and pepper
- 4 boar chops
- 2 tbsp. oil

Whip the butter until soft, add the mustard, Pernod and salt and pepper to taste. Put into plastic wrap and mold into the shape of a cylinder. Place in the freezer for one hour or overnight. Cook the chops quickly in the oil and season each side with salt and pepper after they have browned. Slice the Pernod butter and serve several pats on top of each chop.

FIDDLEHEADS

1 lb. fiddleheads
3 tbsp. unsalted butter
Salt and pepper

Cut the bottoms off the fiddleheads leaving about ¾ of the stem. In a large soup pot or bowl full of cold water soak the fiddleheads for 5 minutes or so. Then, by the handful, rinse the fiddleheads under the faucet. Pour out the potful of water and repeat the process two or three more times or until the brown chaff has been completely removed. It is very important to remove as much of the chaff as possible because it causes the fiddleheads to be bitter. Bring a quart of salted water to boil and drop in just a handful of the fiddleheads. Cook for 3 to 4 minutes or until they're just tender. Scoop them out and plunge them into ice water to stop the cooking. Drain the fiddleheads and dry them on an old towel. Repeat this until you have cooked all the fiddleheads, changing the boiling water with each handful of fiddleheads. Finally, sauté the fiddleheads quickly in the unsalted butter and serve. It's worth it.

RASPBERRY TART

- 1 sheet Pepperidge Farm Puff Pastry or your own (or mine, p.250)
- 1 tbsp. butter
- 2 tbsp. sugar
- ½ pint heavy cream
- ½ tbsp. framboise (the liqueur rather than the raspberry brandy)
- 3 tbsp. sour cream
- 2 pints raspberries
- 2 tbsp. currant jam

Preheat the oven at 425° for at least 20 minutes.

Roll out the pastry and fit into a heavily buttered porcelain tart or quiche dish. Roll the rolling pin over the top to cut the extra pastry off the edges. Let rest in the refrigerator for 1 hour. Prick the pastry with a fork and then flatten a piece of foil tightly over it. Put beans, peas, or pastry weights on top of the foil. Cook in the lower part of the hot oven for 7 minutes then carefully open the oven and remove the foil and weights. Sprinkle with sugar and continue cooking for at least 5 minutes until the crust is a light brown with a shiny, caramelized surface. Then remove from the oven and let cool 1 minute. Slide the pastry out of the dish onto a cake rack to cool completely.

Whip the cream. About half way through whipping add the framboise and the sour cream. Spread over the bottom of the pastry shell. Arrange the raspberries on top of the cream attractively (peaches, blueberries or any fruit are good also). Melt the currant jam over a low flame. Remove and let cool slightly. Add a dash of the liqueur you used in the cream. With a 2-inch pastry brush, paint the raspberries with the jam mixture. Serve immediately as it will become soggy if you try to hold it.

Roast Sheep
Sautéed Watercress
Pasta with Chestnuts and Pignolis
Poached Prunes and Apricots with Cognac and Cream

Serves four

This is one of those menus that whenever I read it I salivate. We had sheep one night on our duck hunting trip in Alaska and the fond memory of it still lingers. Although, in retrospect, I have wondered if this was because we had had Ron Rau's gizzard stew and military c-rations ("coffee, Type II") the previous evening. It is all relative. Nonetheless, the following is a wonderful meal.

ROAST SHEEP

- 3-4 lbs. rolled loin roast
- 2 tbsp. oil
- 2 tbsp. cognac
- 1½ cups veal stock
- 1 garlic clove, chopped
- 4 tbsp. unsalted butter
- Peel from 1 lime, blanched and julienned
- Salt and pepper

Clean any fat off the roast and brush it with the oil. Roast the sheep in a hot 450° oven for 1 to 1½ hours according to your taste. Remove the roast from the pan to a warm serving platter. Deglaze the pan with cognac and then add veal stock, chopped garlic and reduce to ½ the amount. Whisk in butter and lime rind. Season with salt and pepper and serve over sliced sheep.

SAUTÉED WATERCRESS

    3 bunches of watercress, washed and spun dry
3-4 tbsp. unsalted butter
       Salt and pepper

Take each bunch of watercress and cut into 2-inch lengths (the bunches should be cut approximately into thirds). Sauté the watercress in the hot unsalted butter for a second or two then add the lid for two minutes. Remove the lid, season with salt and pepper and a little more butter, and serve.

PASTA WITH CHESTNUTS AND PIGNOLIS

½ lb. chestnuts
¼ cup pignolis
4 tbsp. unsalted butter
1 cup heavy cream
1 tsp. dried sage leaves
½ lb. prepared pasta
   Salt and pepper

Make a deep "X" on the tip of each of the chestnuts and then roast under the broiler till their shells are slightly black and cracked. Let them cool then peel and slice them so you have about ¼ cup of chestnuts. Sauté the pignolis in half of the butter till light brown then add the remaining butter and chestnuts and sauté a bit more. Reduce the cream by letting it boil slowly in a frying pan till it is halved in quantity then add the sage. Cook the pasta, drain and wash, and return it to the cooking pan and toss with the cream. Add the pignolis and chestnuts and check for seasoning.

POACHED PRUNES AND APRICOTS WITH COGNAC AND CREAM

- 12 orange rind slivers
- 12 lemon rind slivers
- 1 bottle of good white wine
- Several whole cloves
- ½ lb. pitted and dried prunes
- ½ lb. dried apricots
- 1 cup cream
- ⅛ cup cognac or Armagnac

Shave an orange and a lemon with a potato peeler making sure not to get any white part of the rind. Put 12 of the shavings from the orange and 12 from the lemon into a pan with the wine and cloves. Bring the mixture to a boil and let simmer for a few minutes. Add the prunes and apricots and let sit for 48 hours or more.

When ready to serve, whip the cream with the cognac in it and serve on top of the fruit.

Braised Rabbit
Sautéed Cucumbers
Red Peppers with Basil
Clafoutis

Serves four

Rabbit is shot and eaten more than any other game in this country. I find it quite good, but often very bony.

BRAISED RABBIT

- 1 rabbit
- 4 tbsp. oil
- 1 carrot, peeled
- 1 small onion
- ½ small celery stick
- 6 parsley stems
- ½ piece bacon or pancetta
- 2 tbsp. unsalted butter
- 1½ cup wine (about)
- 1½ cup stock (about)
- Pinch of thyme
- 1 bay leaf
- 1 pint heavy cream
- 2 tbsp. dried basil
- Salt and pepper

Cut up the rabbit into pieces and brown quickly in the oil. Remove the rabbit from the pan. Chop the carrot, onion, celery, parsley stems and bacon and sauté in the butter. Add the rabbit pieces, except for the breast, and pour enough wine and stock in equal parts to cover ⅔ of the rabbit. Bring this to a boil, turn down to a simmer, add the thyme and bay leaf and cover with aluminum foil, pressing down and fitting it closely to the rabbit and liquid and bringing it over the sides of the pot for a good seal. Continue cooking on simmer until done (about an hour) or when a skewer inserted into the meat comes out clean. The breast meat should be added to the pot about 10-15 minutes before all is done. Meanwhile, in another pan, reduce the pint of cream to 1 cup and add the basil. Season the cream mixture with salt and pepper and set aside. Remove the rabbit pieces to a warmed serving platter and discard the bay leaf. Strain the liquid and return it to the pan to reduce to half its quantity. Add the reduced basil cream and check for seasoning. Season with salt and pepper and pour over the rabbit.

SAUTÉED CUCUMBERS

- 8 cucumbers
- Salt
- 2 tbsp. unsalted butter
- 1 tsp. oil
- Pepper
- Sprinkle of dill

Cut and peel the cucumbers in half lengthwise and scoop out the seeds with a teaspoon. Then cut into ¼-inch slices and place in a colander. Sprinkle with salt and let drain for 40 minutes. Rinse the cucumber in cold water. Meanwhile melt the butter in a frying pan and add the oil. When it is hot, add the cucumber and sauté till just tender. Season with salt, pepper, and the dill.

RED PEPPERS WITH BASIL

- 2 red peppers, seeded and julienned
- 3 tbsp. unsalted butter
- 1 tsp. basil
- ½ tsp. lemon juice
- Salt and pepper

Sauté the red pepper in hot butter for just a minute. Add the basil and lemon juice and toss. Season with salt and pepper.

CLAFOUTIS

- ¾ cup milk
- ½ cup flour
- 1 tsp. vanilla (or grated lemon or orange rind)
  Pinch of salt
- 2 eggs
- ¼ cup granulated sugar
- 1 lb. cherries, pitted (or use any good fruit)
  Confectioners' sugar

Mix the milk, flour, vanilla or rind, salt, eggs and 2 tablespoons of the granulated sugar together. Butter an oven-proof serving dish and pour a third of the batter in it. Bake that for 10 minutes at 375°. Remove from the oven and add the fruit and sprinkle with the remaining sugar. Pour in the rest of the batter and continue cooking in the oven for 30 minutes. Sprinkle with confectioners' sugar and cut into pie-shaped wedges.

Rabbit Salad
Black Olive Bread
Baked Apples with Crème Anglaise

Serves four

RABBIT SALAD

- 1 rabbit
- 2 tbsp. oil
- ¼ cup stock
- 2 tbsp. red wine vinegar
- ¼ cup walnut oil
- 1 shallot, chopped fine
- Salt and pepper
- 2 tbsp. hazelnuts, chopped
- Bittergreen (chicory, escarole, radicchio)

Brush the rabbit with oil and cook in a preheated oven at 350° for about an hour. Remove the rabbit and cut all the meat from the bones and then into bite-size pieces. Now deglaze the pan that the rabbit cooked in with the stock. Turn the heat to low. In a blender, whiz together the vinegar, walnut oil and shallot, taste for salt and pepper, and then add it to the stock in the pan. Toast hazelnuts a few minutes in the oven then wrap in a towel to steam and rub off the skins. Chop coarsely and reserve. Toss the rabbit meat and bittergreens together with the walnut oil and stock mixture. Sprinkle the hazelnuts in and check for salt and pepper. Serve immediately.

BLACK OLIVE BREAD

2 cups lukewarm to warm water
1 tbsp. dry yeast
1 tbsp. sugar
1 tbsp. salt
1 tsp. dried thyme
5 cups all-purpose flour
½ cup pitted black olives, chopped coarsely
Butter or oil for greasing pans

In the bowl of a standing mix master, fitted with a bread hook, add the warm water and sprinkle in the yeast, sugar, salt, and dried thyme. Let sit for a few minutes until the yeast looks dissolved and foamy. Now pour in 5 cups of flour and mix at the lowest setting, usually marked "stir," until the flour is blended and then increase the speed to the next level, #2. Continue blending at this speed until the dough is well mixed, pulling away from the sides of the bowl, and forming a ball. Add the olives to the dough. Turn onto a floured surface and knead the dough for about 8 minutes. It should be slightly tacky to the touch but smooth and very malleable. Place in a bowl that has been oiled, turn the dough over in the oil so the top is oiled, too, and cover the bowl with a cloth. Let rise until it is double in size, about 2 to 3 hours. Punch it down and let it rest while you prepare the pan(s) for it to rise in again.

This recipe makes enough for a baguette and a loaf. I always make a baguette for the week's spaghetti night so I pull a handful of dough off and roll it into a big snake and lay it in one side of a baguette pan that has been buttered. The remaining dough I use to make the Black Olive bread for this menu by forming a ball with the dough, flouring it heavily, and putting it into a banneton, also heavily floured. Both the baguette and the round I cover with a cloth and let rise again for another hour or so.

Using a banneton can be a bit tricky but it produces a beautiful round of bread. Using a piece of parchment paper, floured, atop the back of a cookie sheet, I carefully invert the banneton and let the dough fall out. Often it loses its rise and I let it sit covered for another hour to rise again. Once the round is ready to bake I slide it onto a pizza stone that is in a preheated oven at 420º and bake it and the baguette for 35 to 40 minutes or until golden. Once baked, I turn the baguette out onto a cooling rack and slide the round on the parchment onto the cookie sheet—also onto the rack to cool. Let cool for 30 minutes or so before cutting. If I don't plan to use the baguette that day I wrap it in foil and put it in the freezer to use another day. (It just needs to be taken from the freezer and put in a preheated oven at 350º for 30 minutes or so.) .

BAKED APPLES WITH CRÈME ANGLAISE

    3 tbsp. sugar
       Rind from one orange, blanched and julienned
    ¼ cup raisins soaked in a little warm water until plump
    4 apples
       Pats of butter

For the Crème Anglaise:
    4 yolks
       Pinch of salt
    ¼ cup sugar
    ½ cup milk
    ½ cup cream
    1 tbsp. liqueur (Grand Marnier is good) or vanilla

Bake the apples first. Combine the sugar, orange peel, and raisins together. Core the apples and cut the peel from the top and bottom. Fill each apple with the raisin mixture and dot the top with butter pats. Bake in a preheated oven at 375° for 40 minutes. While the apples cook, make the crème anglaise. Whisk together the yolks, salt and sugar. Combine the milk and cream and whisk that into the yolks. Cook over a medium-high heat stirring constantly until it thickens quite suddenly. Remove from the heat, strain and then whisk till cool. Add the liqueur or vanilla and spoon the crème anglaise over the cooked apples. Can be served hot or cold.

Boar with Ginger and Orange Sauce
Fried Bread
Fried Sage Leaves
Good Floating Island

Serves four

Fried sage leaves sound perhaps peculiar but are a delightful taste sensation. The quantity suggested here is really only a minimum requirement. If you have more large leaves, use them.

BOAR WITH GINGER AND ORANGE SAUCE

      A large sprig of rosemary
4-5 lbs. roast of boar, cleaned of any fat
¼ cup cognac
2 cups stock (preferably veal)
1 orange, juice and rind peeled with a potato peeler (no white pith)
5 tbsp. unsalted butter
2 tsp. fresh ginger, peeled and julienned
    Salt and pepper
    Sprigs of watercress

Put the sprig of rosemary in the bottom of the roasting pan and put the boar on top. Roast the boar for 1½ to 2 hours at 325°. Remove the roast to a warm platter. Remove the rosemary.

Deglaze the pan with cognac, add the veal stock and ½ cup of orange juice (be sure to save the rind from the orange). Reduce the liquid by half all the time whisking it. Add the butter and continue whisking. Blanch and julienne the orange rind. Add ginger, orange rind to the veal stock mixture and remove from the heat. Then add any of the juices from the sliced meat and season with salt and pepper. Serve the boar with the sauce and garnish with watercress.

FRIED BREAD

1 loaf French bread
1 garlic clove
½ cup (1 stick) unsalted butter
   Salt to taste

Slice the French bread into 12 ½-inch pieces and dry them on a cookie sheet in a 300° oven. Do not let them cook. If you wish, rub one side of the dried bread with a garlic clove sliced in half. In a heavy-bottomed saucepan, melt the stick of butter heating it till it sizzles. Put in the bread and brown both sides. Sprinkle with salt if you like.

FRIED SAGE LEAVES

½ cup large sage leaves
2 tbsp. unsalted butter

Fry the sage leaves in butter until they're stiff. Remove with wooden tongs and season with salt. Use as a garnish on or around meat, or as an hors d'oeuvre.

GOOD FLOATING ISLAND

For the custard:
- 12 eggs, separated
- ¼ tsp. salt
- 1 cup sugar
- 3 cups medium cream
- 2 tbsp. vanilla or liqueur (Grand Marnier, Tia Maria or rum are good)

For the islands:
- 12 egg whites
- Pinch of salt
- ½ cup sugar

For the caramel sauce:
- ⅔ cup sugar
- ¼ cup water

To make the custard, whisk together the egg yolks, ¼ teaspoon salt and 1 cup of the sugar until they are just combined. Add the cream and mix well trying not to make any foam. Pour into a heavy-bottomed saucepan and heat over a medium flame. Stir constantly as it will get hot slowly and then thicken quite suddenly. Watch carefully, and as soon you see steam rising from the pot and the custard thickening remove from the heat and pour through a strainer. Whisk till cool. Add the vanilla or liqueur and refrigerate at least an hour. (The custard may be made the day before.)

To make the islands beat the egg whites, with the pinch of salt, until soft peaks are formed. Then add ½ cup sugar and beat until the whites are smooth and stiff.

Now make caramel sauce by putting ⅔ cup sugar and ¼ cup water into a frying pan and cooking over a high heat until it foams and bubbles and becomes a golden caramel. Remove immediately from the heat and use as it will continue to darken and become stiff. If it becomes too hard add a little water and warm over a low heat.

Smooth the custard into a low serving dish and spoon the whites on top in blobs to form the islands. Take a fork and dip it into the caramelized sugar. Crisscross the islands of whites with the caramelized fork, dipping it every time a criss or cross is made.

This dessert can sit finished for about an hour if the egg whites have been beaten enough.

Game Bird Sausage with Rhubarb-Port Syrup
Pasta with Fresh Chanterelles
Sautéed Watercress
Pistachio Gelato

Serves four

Unless you are a very productive hunter, game birds can occasionally pose a problem in the kitchen. One bird, especially the smaller ones like dove, woodcock, or teal don't have an adequate amount of meat to be used for the main course—even for just two people. Often a one-bird hunt, followed by many unsuccessful hunts, requires freezing that one little bird in the hopes of it finding several companions—hopefully the same size—so that all can be cooked together and actually produce a meal for at least two. And even that doesn't always work out—a pheasant, a duck, and a woodcock served together produce enough meat for four, but trying to cook three birds of different size and meat color is tricky at best. So I've included this recipe for game bird sausage to accommodate the potpourri found in your treasure chest of a freezer. Not only is it good for the mixed bird meal but for the frozen-for-a while and the very shot up, not so pretty birds.

Chanterelles are a wild mushroom that more and more can be found fresh in a good grocery store. This is in part because they are easily foraged for—the golden chanterelles have only one poisonous lookalike, the Jack O' Lantern, which is easily discerned when picking since chanterelles do not grow on wood as do the Jack O' Lanterns. Chanterelles are found throughout the United States in oak and conifer and are abundant from midsummer well into the fall in most places. Needless to say, I am not suggesting that if you are a novice you should forage and eat this or any wild mushroom without first getting positive identification from an expert—someone who has picked and eaten wild mushrooms often.

GAME BIRD SAUSAGE WITH RHUBARB-PORT SYRUP

For sausages
- ¾ lb. boneless and skinless breasts, ground or finely chopped
- ¾ lb. ground pork
- 3 tbsp. duck fat
- 3 tbsp. dried cherries, coarsely chopped
- 3 tbsp. ruby port
- 2 tsp. nutmeg
- Salt and white pepper

For the rhubarb port syrup
- ½ cup ruby port
- ½ cup sugar
- 3 cups rhubarb, chopped
- 1 tbsp. pink peppercorns
- Baby Arugula Leaves
- Good green olive oil
- Fleur de sel or kosher salt

Mix game bird breast meat, pork, and duck fat with dried cherries, port, nutmeg and salt and pepper to taste. Check seasonings by frying a little of the mixture. Adjust seasonings if necessary. Place 2 tablespoons of the mixture on a piece of plastic wrap and roll to form sausages, approximately 2 to 3 inches in length. Secure ends with kitchen twine and reserve. Bring a large pot of water to a rolling boil, add sausages and poach 5 minutes, until just cooked through. Remove sausages from water and cool, then store in a tightly wrapped container until ready to use (note—these are best made a day or two ahead).

For syrup, combine port and sugar in a saucepan and simmer until sugar dissolves. Add rhubarb and cook until very soft, approximately 20 minutes. Strain through a fine mesh sieve and pour into clean saucepan. Reduce slowly to a syrup, skimming froth as needed, about 10 minutes. Add peppercorns and reserve at room temperature.

Remove plastic wrap from sausages and cook over medium heat until browned and heated through. Drizzle with rhubarb-port syrup and garnish with baby arugula tossed with the good green olive oil and fleur de sel.

PASTA WITH FRESH CHANTERELLES

    3-4 handfuls of fresh chanterelles (or what you found and think will be enough with the pasta for four)
    1 tbsp. unsalted butter
    1 cup heavy cream
    1 tbsp. fresh sage leaves
    ½ lb. prepared pasta or homemade (see page 43)
       Salt and pepper

Cut off the bottom end of the chanterelle stems and under a running facet rinse each mushroom lightly, brushing off the dirt etc. with a soft mushroom brush. Place mushrooms in a salad spinner and give them a whirl—or let dry a bit on paper towel. Cut any really large mushrooms in half and then put just the chanterelles in a fry pan and turn on high, stir every now and then until all water is evaporated. Add the butter and cook until the mushrooms begin to get soft. Remove from the pan and then reduce the cream by letting it boil slowly in the frying pan till it is halved in quantity then add the sage and the cooked mushrooms, cook a minute more and then set aside. Cook the pasta, drain and rinse, and return it to the cooking pan and toss with the cream and mushroom mixture. Check for seasoning.

SAUTÉED WATERCRESS

    3 bunches of watercress, washed and spun dry
    3-4 tbsp. unsalted butter
       Salt and pepper

Take each bunch of watercress and cut into 2-inch lengths (the bunches should be cut approximately into thirds). Sauté the watercress in the hot unsalted butter for a second or two then add the lid for two minutes. Remove the lid, season with salt and pepper and a little more butter, and serve.

PISTACHIO GELATO

- 4 cups whole milk
- 1 cup sugar
- 3 tbsp. cornstarch
- 2 cups unsalted pistachios, shelled and finely ground
  (Enough ice and salt for processing in your ice cream maker)

Bring 3 cups of the milk to a simmer in a medium-size pan and then remove from the heat. With the remaining cup of milk add the sugar and cornstarch in a bowl and blend in the hot milk, stirring well. Return the milk mixture to the pan and cook, stirring, until it has thickened slightly, about 8 to 10 minutes. Into a bowl place the ground pistachios and pour in the hot, thickened milk mixture. Let it cool and then cover with plastic wrap and place in the frig overnight. Next day strain the mixture through a mesh strainer (the finer the mesh the fewer pieces of pistachio will be in the gelato), push the mixture through the strainer with the back of a wooden spoon, and into the ice-cream maker canister. Throw out the pistachios and process the gelato in the ice cream maker per the manufacturer's instructions.

Game Care

Ed brought home the first deer of our life together—to a Boston apartment. Our small daughter in my arms, we stood on the curb of the city street marveling over the beautiful animal lying across the top of the Jeep. Musing slightly over the incongruity of the situation, I watched as the car disappeared down the dark street bound for the suburban home of a friend where it was to be "hung." And the slow realization came over me: "What now?"

At that point I knew only to worry about the obvious mechanics of how to get a whole carcass into the form of cut-up pieces of meat. What I was to learn subsequently was that what had come before the car-top journey and then the processing of the meat was actually of equal significance and consequence to the quality of the various cuts of meat and how they should be cooked. And worry is what I would have done had I any game care experience back then. That deer had been through a lot by the time it got to Boston.

It was a particularly large whitetail, about 210 pounds field-dressed. Ed had shot it in a very remote area of New Hampshire and worked the better part of a day—along with his hunting companion Larry—just to drag the deer back to camp. But then there was an even greater challenge:

the camp and the deer were on one side of a swollen stream and the car was on the other. Getting the deer across the stream and onto the roof of the car was going to be no easy task. The frail, skinny, rope bridge which dangled above the stream was meant only for a thin-framed human walking single-file and didn't seem the way to go. On the other hand, forging the waist-deep rocky-bottomed stream with the 210 pounds of dead weight seemed, at best, un-fun. Weighing the options carefully, the men struck on a third possibility, a somewhat modified rope and pulley system—or the old wrap around the tree trick—for accomplishing their task of getting the deer cartop.

With Larry on one side of the stream, he fixed a rope to the deer's antlers, and Ed walked the footbridge with the other end of the rope to wrap around a big tree on the opposite side of the stream. The rope could have been fastened securely around the tree, Larry gone to Ed's side of the river, and the two men could have hauled the beast together or even enlisted the muscle of the car. That could have been the way it worked, yes it could have been a plan. But in eager anticipation of Ed's end of the rope being secured, Larry dragged the deer very close, too close, to the stream's edge. Then, in a forceful flash, the stream snatched the carcass, and caused the premature launching of the deer. With the other end of the rope not yet fastened, the deer was afloat and gone! And without those antlers grabbing as it went, the deer would have been gone forever downstream. But the big deer's trophy rack snagged a semi-submerged log and brought Ed plunging mid-stream to wrestle with the antlers, the submerged log, and the current in order to save his great prize. Then there was trying to get the deer on top of the car, and driving it eight hours to Boston. Yes, a lot had happened to this deer and probably it wasn't good, at least in terms of its culinary value.

It was likely the day of being pulled through the woods, the streamside bath, the cold, cold of the water and then the warmer air would not have enhanced the flavor or tenderness of the meat, or could it? While standing curb-side in that city street so long ago, I didn't know enough to care. But today I'd know to consider the trials and tribulations unique to that deer—or duck or pheasant or rabbit—and also to have some other questions for the hunter: Was it a clean shot? Had the critter run (or flown) far after being shot? How long and at what temperature had it lain dead before being field dressed? What was its probable diet and age? What a general pain in the neck I would have made of myself. But all those elements can in fact, or according to folk lore anyway, affect the meat.

What is fact and what is myth? Much has been written in game cookbooks and in the outdoor literature about how different elements, both in the field as well as in the kitchen, affect the taste of game. It always has been very hard for me to discern what is simply the opinion of the writer (or is included more for the sake of tradition) and what is based on fact. I wanted scientific reasons for why venison, partridge, pheasant should be hung—or do they in fact really need to be hung at all—and if so for how long, head up or down, etc. Fortunately, coming from a family of meatpackers and food technologists, I have some sources of scientific information.

My father is a chemical engineer who spent 35 years in the food industry specializing in food processing and meat packing in scores of countries around the world. Here is some of the information he provided about the care and treatment of meat.

About freezing:

Of course, the first consequence of freezing is that it cuts down on bacteria growth and allows us to keep the meat for a long time. At the same time it has several other consequences. Meat has a very high water content—over 65%. Freezing causes the globules of water cells to crystallize. The size of the crystals is in inverse proportion to the speed of freezing. If the freezing occurs quickly the crystals will be quite small. If the freezing happens slowly the crystals will be quite large and cause any yet-unfrozen water to exude out of the meat. In addition, as the temperature is lowered expansion of the water cells occurs and may cause a bursting of the cells if done slowly. Consequently, slow freezing can cause the meat to lose moisture and also become mushy. Slow thawing, as in a refrigerator, may have a similar effect. As the temperature of the refrigerator goes up and down the cells may crystallize and then liquify causing the same bursting and exuding of moisture. The blowers inside frost-free freezers, or any air movement, can cause freezer burn, a desiccation of the meat.

All that this suggests is that if meat is going to be frozen it should be done as quickly as possible, well wrapped and then thawed quickly (or at least at a consistently warm temperature). The suggested wrap for frozen meat is a first layer of aluminum foil to obtain rapid heat transfer and protection from air and then 12 hours later a second wrap of a plastic bag to protect further against air movement. Added tips are to press the foil tightly around the meat. Remember to label with weight, date, and to grade the piece and when the baggie goes over it to suck the air out before the twist-tie goes on. The labeling, of course, helps you know what you're cooking before you've thawed it. Nothing worse than to plan an ooh la la dinner and then discover you've thawed that shot-up shoveler that's been in the freezer a year (almost all meat has significantly deteriorated after a year of the freezer).

About smoking meat:

A hot smoking of meat, like freezing, has the effect of cutting down on the bacteria growth, allowing the meat to be kept longer. Smoking does three things to meat: it heats it, dries it and adds flavor to it. The long, slow heating process of smoking brings the temperature of the meat to above 127° or the "denaturing point." This changes the color of the meat from blood red and kills some, but not all, of the bacteria. The meat also becomes firmer. The drying cuts the moisture content and makes the meat less hospitable to bacteria, while the addition of the smoked flavor adds some acidity, making it even more difficult for certain bacteria to grow. The amount of time a piece of smoked meat can be kept depends largely on the effectiveness of the heating, drying and flavoring process. This may be difficult to determine. Often we don't know much about how well a piece of meat has been smoked or how long it's been hanging around since the smoking. The general guidelines are these: A commercially cured and smoked ham can be kept for up to a year in a cool, dry place; something you smoke yourself in the backyard can probably go as long as a month in the refrigerator and probably six months to a year in the freezer. Fortunately, meat is quite forgiving. And, as my father would say, "it will let you know when it's had it."

About hanging meat:

Hanging meat, or aging it, tenderizes it. The aging process begins after rigor mortis has peaked. Rigor mortis begins a few hours after the animal has been shot and increases very rapidly, peaking at about 10 to 24 hours. It then will decline with the curve flattening at about 48 hours and will continue to decline for two weeks. The meat will be at its toughest stage during rigor mortis and then it will become increasingly more tender. The amount of time for aging to occur is significantly affected by the air temperature. This is why the location of your hunt has a great deal to do with how long the meat should be hung and how it should be handled right after shooting it. In general, the higher the temperature the faster the aging process and the softer the meat. Of course, if the temperature is too high growth of bacteria is promoted, too. Consequently how long an animal should be hung has to do with your own taste buds and the temperature control over the period of aging (a good regulated temperature of 45-50 degrees is optimum).

Taste being the key, it is difficult to advise in such matters. But since much of what is found acceptable is based on what Americans are used to, the guideline for venison might start at what is desirable for beef, and in this country all beef is aged about two weeks.

We basically don't really hang our birds for a specific amount of time, although there are occasions when a whole, in-the-round, and un-plucked bird does sit in the refrigerator for a day or two before it is cleaned. This is essentially like hanging it. However, I haven't really noticed a difference between the flavor of the birds aged in this manner and those that are instantly cleaned and plucked in the field by the guide while you're finishing the hunt. We do age our venison anywhere from a week to two, depending on the weather and how long the temperatures hold steady. This, of course, is the bottom line for us. If not rigged with a cooler, the length of time for aging becomes somewhat a function of what the weatherman dictates and has not much to do with what has been advised or found to be most desirable.

About cleaning the meat:

In our culture the taste of blood is generally not well received and some lengths should be gone to clean the game properly if you wish to comply with cultural norms. Of course, the hunter can always help by trying for a lung shot on the bigger animals such as a deer. The lung shot will guarantee the least amount of damage, blood or otherwise, to the meat, and also kill the animal quickly. Hanging the animal for aging or butchering with the head to the ground is suggested for cleanliness sake. A spraying with water before freezing or refrigeration is also advisable for meat in order to keep down the bacteria count. Use paper towel to pat the meat dry rather than the kitchen dish towel (no need to add the bacteria from the towel back into the meat).

Other things which can affect the flavor of the meat:

Age, size and even sex of the animal can affect the taste. This is especially true of the glandular meat (neck and shoulder meat) in deer. An old, big female is likely to have tougher, stronger flavored neck meat than the saddle from a young, small buck. Age and size also dramatically affect the flavor of game birds

The flavor of whatever the critter has been eating is most intense in the fat and will flavor the meat if left on while cooking. To soak meat in water, salted water, or milk causes some exuding of flavor from the meat. Then, after the exuding, the flavor of the salt and milk will mask what the animal has been feeding on.

The effect of cooking:

The purpose of cooking a piece of meat is to render it more digestible and to eliminate any diseases. The specifics of how something is cooked get into a matter of taste, of course, but certain generalizations can be made. The longer and slower meat is cooked the more tender and easily digestible it becomes (it also loses more of the vitamins). The higher and shorter the heat, the juicier the meat and the crisper the skin. Finally, to cook a bird "in the round" probably does nothing to the taste of the meat. It probably does make the innards more convenient to eat if you like them. One word of caution, however, on this. Innards, particularly the liver, are the body's depository for any number of chemicals that have been ingested by the critter. In this insecticide-laden society that is worth remembering. It is also why the use of nontoxic shot (versus lead) has become mandatory on the duck marsh.

So how do you positively anticipate correctly the taste of your game meat? In short, you can't. You can know that a neck roast from a big, old, bark-eating female deer with blood and fat all over it and cooked ten hours after it was shot or a year after being in the freezer, unwrapped, then cooked on a high heat for a long time will taste like shoe leather. But hopefully you knew that before you read this. Every time an element is altered, the taste is altered. And what must be kept in perspective are those elements which you have some control over. Hopefully the generalized facts listed above which determine flavor and texture will help you determine what things you are going to strive to control. It is possible to control the temperature for hanging by purchasing your very own $10,000 meat locker. It is possible to break the law and shoot a springtime buck. It is possible to eat only the saddle roast from a deer dead one hour. All these things are possible, but often impractical or illegal or un-fun. Focus on what suits you to control and beware of the risks when you do cut corners. Certainly the height of control is to make the meat into what we eat every day: created, maintained, slaughtered and packaged meat with a predictable flavor. Hopefully the adventurous spirit in you is willing to try to eat and cook what the hunter presents. Be smart and energetic when preserving and cooking game, but also willing to improvise when a lack of ideal circumstances dictates it.

Lastly, remember that in the final analysis what often constitutes proper game care is usually linked to what makes the meat taste "good." And what constitutes "good" in taste is not always agreed upon.

There's More to a Menu Than the Game

Many times the design of my menus has more to do with the chaos that is occurring in my life that day or the ingredients I have on hand or what my mood might dictate. If I have been hunting all day and want a fast, easy game meal, I might choose one set of recipes over the ones that I save for the Annual Event or for the intimate candle-lit dinner for two. This is true, I believe, of all of us. So I have re-shuffled all the menus in the preceding chapters and list them here in accordance with the occasion.

Menus for After a Day of Hunting

Or whatever it is that is filling your day. These are, for the most part, quick and easy menus. Planned for immediate assembly, or for making ahead. But take care because several of the ingredients may not be something that you casually stock.

Grilled Venison Chops with Blue Cheese and Caraway Seeds
Sweet Potato Gratin
Braised Fennel
Fresh Figs

Venison Scallops
Persillade Potatoes
Green Beans
Tarte Tatin

Duck Roasted with Red Pepper Butter
Persillade Potatoes
Sautéed Green Beans and Cherry Tomatoes
Almond Cake

Stuffed Duck Breasts
Green Beans with Wild Mushrooms
Bibb and Radish Salad
Grapefruit Sabayon

Woodcock Armagnac
Fennel and Peas
Roast Potatoes
Garlic Toasts
Tarte Tatin

Duck with Ginger and Scallions
Sautéed Watercress
Cheese, Thyme Toast
Chocolate Cake

Venison Strip Steaks
Fried Potato Skins
Red Pepper Salad
Strawberry Ice Cream

Sea Duck With Pancetta and Prosciutto
Roast Potatoes with Rosemary
Fresh Green Peas
Kiwi Ice

Quail Soup
Pasta with Chestnuts and Pignolis
Olive Oil and Salt Bread

Spitted Woodcock
Green Beans with Wild Mushrooms
Meyer Lemon Sherbet

Grilled Quail
Purée of Peas
Grilled Mushrooms
Pear Cake

Menus for the Great Outdoors

Several of these menus, with some minor adaptation, could be suitable for the first or second night out on a camping trip. They are not the filler-up-fuel type meals but rather the kind which celebrate the beginning of a hunting trip. Consider carefully, as some of the recipes call for a fair amount of refrigerated food and your cooler may not be able to handle it on a particular trip. Or some may simply be more suitable for the evening back at home, standing with cocktail in hand over the barbecue and gazing off, remembering the trip past.

Grilled Venison Steaks with Rosemary Butter
Bibb Lettuce and Tomato Salad
White Bean Purée
Coffee Ice Cream with Hazelnut Liqueur

Venison Steaks with Wild Mushrooms
Blue Cheese Polenta
Spinach and Bibb Lettuce Salad
Strawberry Ice

Grilled Breast of Duck with Wild Mushrooms
    and Honey Mustard Sauce
Olive Oil and Salt Bread
Soup in a Pumpkin
Figs in Rum

Grilled Breast of Mallard
Gorgonzola Polenta
Cucumbers and Radishes
Fresh Fruit

Quick Grilled Quail
Cauliflower with Mayonnaise
Sautéed Watercress
Chocolate Cake

Pheasant and Ruffed Grouse Sandwiches
Cold Wild Rice Salad
Assorted Cheeses
Olives
Fresh Fruit

Grouse Pancetta
Julienned Celery and Zucchini
Fried Polenta
Poached Prunes and Apricots with Cognac and Cream

Quail for the Campfire
Grilled Red Onion
Grilled Bread
Almond Cake

Menus That Are Ooh La La

No matter how much game you shoot, it is always special. These menus are for the silver, the game plates, the linen, the cognac and, in general, for making life a little bit more elegant.

Boar with Ginger and Orange Sauce
Fried Bread
Fried Sage Leaves
Good Floating Island

Venison with Port
Roast Potatoes
Sautéed Watercress
Meyer Lemon Sherbet

Preserved Woodcock with Olives
Basil Pasta
Sun-dried Tomato Bread
Cantaloupe Ice

Roast Wild Turkey
Fontina Polenta
Fava Beans, Peas, and Pancetta
Green Salad
Rhubarb Tart

Smoked Goose Salad
Butternut Squash Soup
Sun-dried Tomato Bread
Chocolate Cake

Christmas Goose Anytime
Pignolis and Raisin Cognac Stuffing
Cornsticks
Sautéed Bittergreens
Good Floating Island

Saddle of Venison
Potatoes and Porcini
Braised Fennel
Clafoutis

Roast Leg of Goat
Blue Cheese Polenta
Mixed Green Salad
Alice Waters' Olive Oil and Sauternes Cake

Boar Chops with Pernod and Mustard Butter
Gaufrette Potatoes
Fiddleheads
Raspberry Tart

Roasted Sheep
Sautéed Watercress
Pasta with Chestnuts and Pignolis
Poached Prunes and Apricots with Cognac and Cream

Menus for People Who Have Never Eaten Game and Don't Eat Things That Walk Sideways or Grow in the Dark

In general, it is probably a bad idea to serve game to the untested palate. Certainly there is nothing so depressing as serving a perfect little grouse just to have it slipped to the dog or shoved under the mashed potatoes. However, there are unavoidable occasions when the unexpected guest arrives after the evening's meal has been pulled from the freezer or when you simply must cater first to your own desires and the guests be hanged. These menus are for those occasions. They will either mask slightly the game taste or utilize the more familiar game that the novice will feel comfortable eating.

Venison Calzone
Sliced Tomatoes with Basil
Fried Sage Leaves
Poached Pears

Venison Steak with Red Wine
Bittergreens and Cheese Salad
Garlic Toasts
Rhubarb Tart

Venison Steaks Marinated
Grilled Red Pepper Salad
Mashed Potatoes with Fresh Basil
Vanilla Ice Cream with Homemade Butterscotch Sauce

Venison Stew with Artichoke Hearts and Sun-dried Tomatoes
Basil Bread
Green Salad
Custard Oranges

Venison Burgers with Chateaubriand Butter
Fried Bread
Vegetable Salad
Fresh Fruit

Game Bird Sausage with Rhubarb-Port Syrup
Pasta with Fresh Chanterelles
Sautéed Watercress
Pistachio Gelato

Marinated Duck Breasts
Plain Roast Potatoes
Julienned Celery and Zucchini
Strawberry Tart

Grilled Marinated Ducks
Grilled Red Onion
Grilled Mushrooms
Basil Bread
Crème Brulée

Pheasant Salad
Soup in a Pumpkin
Basil Bread
Figs in Rum

Roasted Duck
Potatoes Steamed with Sage
Bittergreens and Cheese Salad
Tangerine Sorbet

Juniper Encrusted Woodcock in Rosemary Cream Sauce
Leg of Lamb
White Bean Purée
Green Salad
Stuffed Oranges

Just for the Two of You

In our hunting careers there have been times when all that the season produced was a meal for two. We plan an evening of candlelight, a late dinner and a very expensive bottle of wine suited to our precious piece of game. Other seasons the meals for two continue, even if we shoot enough for a party.

Venison Chops with Basil Cream
Homemade Pasta with Parsley
Salad with Hazelnut Dressing
Brandied Apricots and Crème Anglaise

Venison Chops with Mustard Butter
Roast Potatoes with Rosemary
Green Beans and Beet Salad
Coffee Granita

Venison Chops with Pignolis and Red Peppers
Pepperoni Bread
Green Salad
Stuffed Oranges

Grilled Lemon Duck
Grated Zucchini
Sautéed Cherry Tomatoes
Grilled Bread
Pear Cake

Minted Roast Duck, Carrots and Turnips
Green Salad
Alice Waters' Olive Oil and Sauternes Cake

Ducks with Rosemary and Sage
Fontina Polenta
Zucchini Fans with Tomatoes
Coffee Ice Cream with Hazelnut Liqueur

Chukar Stuffed with Hazelnuts

Grated Zucchini
Sautéed Cherry Tomatoes
Cheese, Thyme Toast
Fresh Fruit

Pheasant in Wine
Fiddleheads
Baked Grits
Strawberry Tart

Green Grape Quail
Wild Rice with Walnuts
Sliced Tomatoes with Basil
Crème Brulée

Dove Salad
Cornsticks
Tangerine Sorbet

And to Feed an Army or Hunting Party ...

These menus suggest what types of game are best suited for feeding a big group. No sense in saving up for six hunting seasons trying to have enough woodcock to feed the skeet club when there's a deer in the freezer.

Braised Bear
Baby Artichokes
Fava Beans, Peas, and Pancetta
Fresh Fruit

Rabbit Salad
Black Olive Bread
Baked Apples with Crème Anglaise

Braised Rabbit
Sautéed Cucumbers
Red Peppers with Basil
Clafoutis

Venison Stew
Homemade Pasta
Crusted Blueberry and Cream Cake

Venison Black Bean Chili
Baby Spinach and Arugula Salad with Avocado and Egg
Fennel Seed Bread
Ginger Angel Crisps

Smoked Goose in Cold Pasta Salad
Pepperoni Bread
Almond Cake

Sea Duck Fricassee
Fennel, Mint, Cucumber, Radish Salad
Fried Polenta
Fresh Fruit

Duck Salad
Basil Pasta
Cantaloupe Ice

Grilled Sea Ducks
Grilled Vegetables
Garlic Cheese Bread
Poached Pears

Pheasant and Cabbage
Cooked Apples
Cheese

Fried Dove
Zucchini with Tomato
Gorgonzola Polenta
Toll House Cookies

A Few Suggestions

When I first started to consult cookbooks for my game dinners, I automatically skipped over this type of chapter. After all, I knew how to cook and I could see on their list of necessary utensils such items as "pepper grinder." How obvious is that, what an insult! Of course, a few game dinner failures would send me lurking into the bathroom, four game cookbooks at a time, to surreptitiously read every "tips" section I could lay my hands on.

Certainly much of what has been said in this book is not revolutionary or even that enlightening. Many of the non-game recipes are repeated in several places throughout the book—because this really is all about the game recipes after all—but several of the suggestions are repeated more than once, too. I did this because I believe people read cookbooks differently than other types of books. Cookbooks are often browsed, pages flipped back and forth, and often the reader starts reading from the back—with the index. If you are like me you have used recipes, maybe a whole menu here and there, long before bothering to read any of the long text. So for the reader like myself there are the quick suggestions woven around the edges of each menu. And for those who actually read a cookbook and do so while standing on one leg in the bookstore or in bed before turning the lights off—or for all of us who have those insecure moments when you panic and will read anything with the word "game" in it—this chapter is for you.

First and foremost, please take note that in the acquisition of all ingredients, not just the game, I, like most hunters, do not scrimp on either time or money. One fall, now some twenty-five years ago, we faced the duck hunting season without a dog. Our five-year-old golden had died suddenly and mysteriously of a kidney ailment during the summer months leaving us without a trained retriever for duck fetching. Quite cleverly, I simultaneously was six months pregnant with our third child and was too fat to wear waders. Ed was left to partake in duck season by himself. He arrived home later than usual one morning with one black duck in hand, slightly chagrined, and very wet. He explained that he'd stripped down to his nothingness on the marsh and dived into the icy water in order to retrieve the beyond-wader-reach bird. We do go to great lengths.

It is important for the cook to remember what has gone before. Cold and wet and fatigue and time—and life and death—are forever part of it. To become cavalier is at best tactless. Ordering up the really good green olive oils in advance, making the veal stock from scratch, watering the sage plant every week, spending the extra dollars on liqueurs are our part of it. And if it seems at times to be too much for too little, just be happy you don't have to jump bare into icy water during October to swim for the duck.

Game dinners can't always be planned well in advance. When the first bird of the season has been shot and it seems sacrilege to freeze it, this is not the time to start ordering walnut oil from a catalog or searching your gourmet shops for dried porcini mushrooms. Certainly alongside the importance of practicing good techniques should be the emphasis on also using good ingredients—you've already started with the best of ingredients, the game, so don't screw that up by using substitute or lesser ingredients in the recipe. The time and money is worth it for bettering the meal and is the very least a cook can do. Remember, the hunter has probably spent three times the money and time to get the critter to the kitchen than you have by stocking good brandy.

For me the pre-hunting season becomes a time for "laying in" supplies and "putting up" homemade items to assist when preparing game and their appropriate side dishes. This preparation will also make the cooking of game menus much easier.

Here are some things to buy and keep around:

Fresh herbs—Buy the little plants that come in cheap plastic containers for a few dollars and use the leaves without care or worry to the health of the plant. When the leaves are gone, buy another plant.

Dried wild mushrooms—Most good grocery stores and certainly gourmet shops have them and their earthy taste goes much better with the flavor of game than the rubbery fresh mushrooms found in grocery stores.

Unsalted butter—Salt is used to mask flavor. We don't want to mask flavor and don't need to add salt to the diet—better to use unsalted butter.

Birds Eye Tender Tiny Peas—They are almost as good as the fresh ones and can be used in many dishes.

Good cooking oils—A good, green olive oil, a walnut or a hazelnut oil are good oils and can be purchased through catalogs, gourmet shops, and good grocery stores. The walnut oil and hazelnut oils will go rancid if you don't use them up after five months or so. Since it is expensive it might be worth finding a friend to split a bottle with.

Sun-dried tomatoes—These are so wonderful and have so many uses, they're worth having on hand throughout the year. They can be found—both the dried version and then packed in oil (much pricier) now in grocery stores as well as gourmet shops.

Wild rice—Wild rice is a classic with game and always a good idea to have around. I don't care for the mixed brown and wild rice, but this is a matter of taste.

Interesting liqueurs and brandy—They will turn a dull item into something very interesting and are fun to play with.

Juniper berries—These seem to be listed in every game cookbook and are among the items I think are definitely worth laying in especially for upland bird recipes.

Duck fat and duck demi-glace—Both are very useful for making game sauces and pan-frying game. The fat and the demi-glace can be difficult to get—but a good grocery store should be able to order it for you or you can get it online at www.Dartagnan.com

Pepperidge Farm Pastry Sheets—This is the best store-bought pastry dough. But still will not compare to well-made, homemade pastry. The problem, of course, with homemade pastry is that it's often a bit tricky to handle—and when it doesn't work it really doesn't work. When I was learning pastry in cooking school, one of my discouraged classmates in exasperation left her pastry "homework"—a small grey disk of tough dough—at the teacher's doorstep, rang the bell and bolted. No one ever 'fessed up to the sad attempt at pastry, but we had our suspicions—and sympathized. It's hard to make!

Galette dough. Over the years I have learned a few tricks and come also to rely on my favorite chef and cookbook writer of all time, Alice Waters, for good pastry recipes. I am especially fond of the galette dough, which she says came originally from Jacques Pépin. It isn't as elegant as her puff pastry—but it does have almost as much butter and is nearly foolproof to make. So below is Jacques'/Alice's recipe now with some of my small additions for producing, well, a reliably good tart.

GALETTE DOUGH

- 2 cups unbleached, all-purpose flour
- 1 tsp. sugar
- ¼ tsp. salt
- 12 tbsp. unsalted butter (1½ sticks), chilled and cut into ½-inch pieces
- 7 tbsp. ice water

In the bowl of a standing mix master, fitted with a pastry blender (not the whisk attachment) combine the flour, sugar, and salt. Add in 4 tablespoons of the cold butter slices and mix until the flour mixture resembles course cornmeal. Then add in the remaining stick of butter slices and blend just until the biggest pieces of butter look like large peas—or a bit larger. Remove the bowl from the mixer and bit by bit—a tablespoonful at a time—add the cold water. After each addition of water toss the mixture, letting it fall through your fingers. Try not to squeeze the dough together or you'll overwork it, making it tough. Keep tossing the dough until it begins to look ropey and is coming together. It will have some dry patches, and if there are more dry patches than rope, add more water. Lay two big pieces of plastic wrap on the counter and form the dough into two rough balls. Place each ball on a piece of the plastic wrap and fold the wrap over the ball, pushing the dough together, and then flattening it into a 4-inch disk. Refrigerate for at least 30 minutes before rolling out. (The dough disk can also be frozen at this point for a few weeks.)

Working with one of the dough disks at a time, take it from the fridge and let it soften. In the meantime, cut a large piece of parchment paper, big enough to accommodate a 14-inch round of pastry dough, and dust it lightly with flour. When the dough has softened remove the wrap and place the disk on the parchment. Flour the top lightly and pinch the edges of the dough so there are no cracks. Now place two sheets of plastic wrap, over-lapping, over the dough and roll it out, pressing as you go at first, then just rolling it to about a 14-inch circle and an ⅛ inch or less thick. Slide the dough/parchment paper onto the back side of a big cookie sheet and put in the refrigerator for a half hour or more before using. Each disk is enough for one open tart.

Here are some things to make and keep around:

Veal stock—It is worth it, it is worth it, it is worth it. Veal stock would probably make horse meat taste good. It rarely can be bought and you have to make it. It can be frozen.

Chicken stock—Although chicken stock can be bought, it is better homemade; it has less salt for one thing. If you must buy chicken stock and live in an area where College Inn brand is available, I recommend it.

Jellies—Good homemade jellies add not only an oft-needed taste but style to an otherwise flat game dinner. Two of my favorites are beach plum and rose hip.

Breads—Having homemade herb bread around can do the same as the homemade jellies—really add class to the meal. Squishy white bread does not seem to have the same effect.

Compound butter—Several different compound butters are listed in this book and all can be kept in the freezer for at least a couple weeks. They are good for those last-minute attempts at making a dinner ooh la la. Also, provides a good vehicle for freezing some of the hard-to-get fresh herbs.

Homemade mayonnaise—This is good to have on hand to use on leftover game.

MAYONNAISE

    1 tbsp. vinegar
    2 tsp. prepared mustard
    ½ tsp. salt
    ½ tsp. ground pepper
    3 egg yolks
    2 cups olive oil

In a bowl put vinegar, mustard, salt and pepper. Whisk to dissolve the salt. Add the egg yolks and whisk 1 minute till frothy. Add the oil very slowly, in dribbles, whisking all the while. Dribble the oil in for at least the first ¼ cup. You may add it faster as the mayonnaise thickens. If the mixture is too thick, add a little hot water to thin. This will also slightly poach the eggs and keep the mayonnaise from separating. When all is combined you have a mayonnaise which now can be seasoned to your own taste. Adjust the salt, pepper and mustard. It is now mayonnaise and you may consider adding lemon juice, herbs, parsley or watercress. Be sure to combine any added herbs in warm water as they will not dissolve in all that oil.

What equipment to obtain is, I believe, truly a personal decision. In general terms I don't believe in purchasing expensive equipment until the level of use warrants the cost. It irritates me when I watch professional cooks on television talk about how to poach a salmon when they are casually heaving around their 3½-foot long poacher. Very few people have a 3½-foot long poacher or the stove to accommodate it, a place to store it, or much less the wherewithal to purchase such an item, especially when it is used once every five years, if you're lucky. Better the TV cook should tell us how to poach a big fish in the turkey roaster. There are a few items, however, which are important to know about because of their particular usefulness with game. Here they are:

Good poultry shears—These are an incredibly valuable item not only for prepping birds or cutting up cooked birds but for cleaning a bird (cuts off feet and neck/head). Invest in a good pair and they will last forever.

Strawberry huller—These are nice little pinchers that are designed to pull the green tops off strawberries, but actually seem better suited to pulling the pinfeathers out of early-season ducks. Necessary only if you don't have good strong fingernails.

Small roasting pans—In general, meat cooks better in a pan which nicely accommodates it, not too big or small. One woodcock in a turkey roaster doesn't work well at all. Since many game birds are smaller than grocery store birds it may be necessary to acquire an especially small roasting pan.

Good sharp knives—A good set of very sharp knives sounds like the pepper grinder suggestion. But I cannot overemphasize how much more pleasant working on a piece of meat can be if done with a variety of sizes of sharp knives that are well suited to your hand. When John Hewitt came to visit, his house present was to sharpen my knives and no better present could there be.

Parchment paper and plastic wrap—Both of these items you likely have on hand anyway, but are very useful for all the breads and pastry-making that is included in this book and goes on in hunting season. I use the plastic wrap to cover pastry when I roll it out—don't have to smother it in flour that way—to prevent sticking. And I also use the parchment paper (lightly floured) for pastry to prevent sticking and also if it is free-standing and doesn't go in a dish, just on a pizza stone to cook; likewise for breads.

Meat grinders—Many game cookbooks contain recipes for venison sausage or ground venison burger but don't really talk about how to grind the meat. I spent one whole evening till 12:30 at night trying to get venison through my handy-dandy hand-crank meat grinder. I think I ended up in tears, but I learned several things. I had chosen to grind the mediocre leg and upper neck pieces which contained a great deal of sinew. A logical choice since those cuts are not good for much else. But just as we would have a difficult time chewing that meat so did the grinder. A big meat locker operation has a machine which actually removes the sinew first. Using a better cut of meat which has never been frozen, but is very cold—nearing frozen—when you grind it makes it much easier. (The beef or pork fat you blend in with the meat should likewise be very cold when you grind it.) I'd also nix the hand crank and buy the meat grinder attachment to your mixer, hand chop the meat, or put it in the food processor for a few quick pulses. Or better still, con some butcher into doing it for you—like those game cookbook writers do.

Smokers—Now that I have said that I don't appreciate books and professional cooks recommending cooking methods which require expensive equipment, I will make the exception. I think smokers are great fun for cooking game and I suggest buying one even if you can't see using it very much. Yes, yes I say don't buy until you're sure of the amount of usage the equipment will get, and we all do own twice as much stuff as we need. But smokers add an entirely new dimension to the taste of game (unlike such items as an electric plucker), can double as an outdoor grill and be used for other than game meat. I think you'll find it is used more than anticipated.

Pasta machines—If you like making your own pasta, a hand-crank machine that kneads and cuts it is indispensible. I use the classic Atlas—made in Italy, of course.

Words of caution to bear in mind about two good pieces of equipment:

Food processors—These handy machines should be used sparingly on starches, only an occasional zip here, zip there. They can break down starches so they are liquified and lose any thickening capability. This is especially important to keep in mind when making a soup where rice or pasta is used specifically to thicken.

Ovens cook very differently. You, undoubtedly, have heard this before, but I have been particularly reminded of it when setting the cooking times for the recipes in this book. I almost had a row with my cooking instructor over the cooking time for crème brulée due (I think) to the differences in our ovens. She kept reiterating that crème brulée is to be just barely firm, not, as some chefs suggest, pudding-like. I knew that, but my cooking time was still 10 minutes longer than she had suggested in the recipe and I found it nearly impossible to caramelize the brown sugar on top. I've cooked in ovens that take a long time to heat up, that don't retain the heat, and never get super hot. Of course all these factors affect the total amount of time, the outcome, and underscore the necessity of preheating and using an auxiliary thermometer if your oven doesn't tell you when it's reached temperature.

Once the suitable ingredients and equipment are assembled there are those happy moments in the kitchen. There are also those unhappy moments in the kitchen. I always feel particularly bad when a game dinner doesn't turn out right. It seems such a waste. But everyone, yes everyone, has failures. Just pretend that the "failure" was actually something you meant to do and that with a little doctoring it will be as good, or better, than the original recipe. Unfortunately, some of my failures have been beyond retrieval. To aid in the prevention of failure, remember the following:

To insure good flavor stuff and truss game birds. They just don't have enough fat content to be cooked with an open cavity.

Stuffing a bird has the effect of putting a sponge in it. If the stuffing is dry, juices will be sucked from the bird. This may be desirable if the bird was poorly cleaned or particularly bloody. If the stuffing is very moist it can add juices. Unless the bird's cavity was immaculately clean, I suggest eating stuffing that has been cooked separately.

Game continues to cook after it has been removed from the heat. This is, of course, true of all things, but particularly true of the high-in-protein, low-in-fat ratio of game.

A good rule of thumb is the smaller the bird the higher the oven temperature.

Doneness. Precisely because ovens do vary in their cooking characteristics, it is wise to learn to determine the doneness of meat by touch (springiness when pressed or looseness of a leg), smell (you know when it's beginning to burn) and sight (coloring and nice oozing juices). To rely on a recipe's stated time for cooking should be for the purpose of determining an approximate length for the cocktail hour and not much more.

Salt and pepper are more effective as flavoring if added after cooking.

Simmering is the waltz, boiling the polka. You should see only an occasional bubble when simmering.

You can always cook something more, but not less.

To "butterfly" a bird is to do this:

What you want to achieve here is a flattened bird with a uniform thickness. First cut out the backbone entirely, then bend the legs and wings as illustrated and insert the leg ends into two slits you have cut just below the breast meat. Press down on the entire bird to flatten. There should be no need to snap the keel bone in a smaller bird.

The purpose of butterflying is to make the cooking speedier and more even.

Pen-raised isn't wild. Many general cookbooks that contain game recipes are often referring to pen-raised game rather than wild game. The techniques and cooking times are in certain cases quite different from the pen-raised to the wild and this should be accounted for—ducks and geese most noticeably so; the pen-raised variety are fatty and often very greasy. This is not true of a wild duck or goose.

Hold the heat. For some reason game more than other meat seems to cool down very quickly so it is particularly important to serve game on heated plates and platters.

Portion control. Serving a reasonably sized portion arranged in a careful and pretty fashion on the plate is one of those signs that indicate you know what you're doing.

Many fine and long-time hunters never truly become able to devise their own, untested hunting experience. They are perfectly capable of hiring the guides so they can follow them through the woods, pull the trigger and kill the bird. It is becoming a rarer commodity to find the hunter who can figure out new territory to hunt and consistently have some relative success on his own in the field. This ability takes much time for sure; I have yet to accomplish it. Certainly, too, there are many fine cooks that produce wonderful meals by simply following the recipes. But for me the greatest fun is in the new creation, the improvised and the successful experiment. It is also why the nature of game cooking—unstructured, unpredictable, and full of room to create—is so exciting to me. I only hope that my excitement is yours, too.

Index

Alice Waters' Olive Oil and Sauternes Cake, 169, 170, 204, 206, 241, 244
Almond Cake, 88, 89, 171, 172, 193, 195, 238, 240, 246
Assorted Cheeses, 114, 240

Baby Artichokes, 207, 208, 245
Baby Spinach and Arugula Salad with Avocado and Egg, 28, 30, 246
Baked Apples with Crème Anglaise, 219, 221, 245
Baked Goat Cheese, 96, 98
Baked Grits, 120, 122, 245
Basil Bread, 46, 48, 130, 132, 162, 164, 242, 243
Basil Pasta, 104, 105, 158, 160, 241, 246
Bear
  Braised, 207
Bibb and Radish Salad, 156, 238
Bibb Lettuce and Tomato Salad, 67, 239
Birds Eye peas, 249
Bittergreens and Cheese Salad, 71, 72, 166, 168, 242, 243
Black Olive Bread, 219, 220, 245
Blue Cheese Polenta, 60, 61, 204, 205, 239, 241
Boar
  Chops with Pernod and Mustard Butter with Ginger and Orange Sauce, 222
Boar Chops with Pernod and Mustard Butter, 210, 241
Boar with Ginger and Orange Sauce, 222, 240
Braised Bear, 207, 208, 245
Braised Fennel, 36, 38, 69, 70, 237, 241
Braised Rabbit, 216, 245
Brandied Apricots and Crème Anglaise, 244

Brandied Apricots with Crème Anglaise, 77, 79
Bread
  Basil, 46, 48, 130, 132, 162, 164, 242, 243
  Black Olive, 219, 220, 245
  Charcoal Grilled, 88, 89
  Fennel Seed, 28, 30, 246
  Fried, 33, 34, 222, 223, 240, 243
  Garlic Cheese, 152, 153, 246
  Grilled, 185, 187, 240, 244
  Olive Oil and Salt, 110, 112, 178, 180, 238, 239
  Pepperoni 54, 55, 193, 194, 244, 246
  Sun-dried Tomato, 104, 106, 188, 190, 191, 241
Butter, compound, 251
Butter, unsalted, 249
Butterflying, 255
Butternut Squash Soup, 188, 190, 241
Butterscotch, homemade, 66

Cantaloupe Ice, 104, 107, 158, 161, 241, 246
Cauliflower with Mayonnaise, 127, 128, 240
Charcoal Grilled Bread, 88, 89
Cheese, Thyme Toast, 139, 141, 146, 147, 238, 245
Chez Panisse Menu Cookbook, 169
Child, Julia, 25
Chocolate Cake, 127, 128, 146, 148, 188, 192, 238, 240, 241
Chocolate Gelato, 86, 87
Christmas Goose Anytime, 196, 241
Chukar. *See under* Upland Birds
Chukar Stuffed with Hazelnuts, 139, 245
Clafoutis, 36, 38, 216, 218, 241, 245
Cold Wild Rice Salad, 114, 116, 240

Cooked Apples, 134, 135, 196, 198, 246
Cookies and Cheese, 114
Cornsticks, 100, 101, 196, 198, 241, 245
Coffee Granita, 57, 59, 244
Coffee Ice Cream with Hazelnut Liqueur, 67, 149, 239, 244
Crème Anglaise, 76, 77, 79, 219, 221
  recipe, 221
Crème Brulée, 162, 165, 243, 245
Crusted Blueberry and Cream Cake, 42, 44, 246
Cucumber and Radishes, 154
Cucumbers and Radishes, 239
Custard Oranges, 46, 49, 110, 113, 242

D'Artagnan, 20
de La Reynière, Grimod, 83
Demi-glace, duck, 249
Doneness, 255
Dove. *See under* Upland Birds
Dove Salad, 100, 245
Duck. *See under* Water Fowl
Duck Roasted with Red Pepper Butter, 171, 238
Duck Salad, 158, 159, 246
Duck with Ginger and Scallions, 146, 238
Duck with Pancetta and Prosciutto, 176
Ducks with Rosemary and Sage, 149, 150, 244
Dumas, Alexandre, 85

Fat, duck, 249
Fava Beans, Peas, and Pancetta, 117, 118, 207, 209, 241, 245
Fennel and Peas, 136, 137, 238
Fennel Seed Bread, 28, 30, 246
Fennel, Mint, Cucumber, Radish Salad, 173, 174, 246
Fiddleheads, 120, 122, 210, 211, 241, 245
Figs in Rum, 130, 133, 178, 181, 239, 243
Fontina Polenta, 117, 118, 149, 151, 241, 244
Food processors, 254
Fresh Figs, 69, 237
Fresh Fruit, 33, 114, 139, 154, 173, 207, 239, 240, 243, 245, 246
Fresh Green Peas, 176, 238
Fried Bread, 33, 34, 222, 223, 240, 243

Fried Dove, 102, 246
Fried Polenta, 173, 175, 240, 246
Fried Potato Skins, 39, 40, 238
Fried Sage Leaves, 74, 75, 222, 223, 240, 242

Galette Dough, 250
Game Bird Sausage with Rhubarb-Port Syrup, 225, 243
Game birds, cooking, basics, 83
Game Care, 229
  cleaning, 233
  effect of cooking, 234
  freezing, 231
  hanging, 232
  other factors, 234
  smoking, 232
Garlic Cheese Bread, 152, 153, 246
Garlic Toasts, 71, 72, 238, 242
Gaufrette Potatoes, 210, 241
Ginger Angel Crisps, 28, 32, 246
Good Floating Island, 196, 199, 222, 224, 240, 241
Goose. *See under* Water Fowl
Gorgonzola Polenta, 102, 103, 154, 155, 239, 246
Grapefruit Sabayon, 156, 157, 238
Grated Zucchini, 139, 140, 185, 186, 244, 245
Gray's Sporting Journal, 18, 23, 60
Gray's Wild Game Cookbook, 17, 20, 21
Green Beans, 52, 57, 58, 237, 238, 244
Green Beans and Beet Salad, 57, 58, 86, 244
Green Beans with Wild Mushrooms, 96, 98, 156, 157, 238
Green Grape Quail, 245
Green Salad, 46, 54, 108, 117, 169, 241, 242, 243, 244
Grilled Bread, 185, 187, 240, 244
Grilled Breast of Duck with Wild Mushrooms, 239
Grilled Breast of Duck with Wild Mushrooms and Honey Mustard Sauce, 178
Grilled Breast of Mallard, 154, 239
Grilled Breast of Sandhill Crane, 86
Grilled Lemon Duck, 185, 244
Grilled Marinated Ducks, 162, 243

Grilled Mushrooms, 124, 125, 162, 163, 239, 243
Grilled Quail, 124, 127, 239, 240
Grilled Red Onion, 88, 162, 163, 240, 243
Grilled Red Pepper Salad, 39, 40, 62, 65, 242
Grilled Sea Ducks, 152, 246
Grilled Vegetables, 152, 246
Grilled Venison Chops with Blue Cheese and Caraway Seeds, 237
Grilled Venison Steak with Rosemary Butter, 67
Grilled Venison Steaks with Rosemary Butter, 239
Grouse. *See under* Upland Birds
Grouse Pancetta, 240

Hazelnut liqueur, 67
Hazelnut Salad, 79
Hirsheimer, Christopher, 20
Homemade Pasta, 42, 43, 77, 78, 244, 246
  recipe, 43
Homemade Pasta with Parsley, 77, 78, 244

Joy of Cooking, 20, 93, 108, 207
Julienned Celery and Zucchini, 182, 183, 240, 243
Juniper berries, 249
Juniper Encrusted Woodcock in Rosemary Cream Sauce, 108, 243

Kiwi Ice, 176, 177, 238
Knives, sharp, 253

Lacey Act, 24, 26
Larousse Gastronomique, 83
Leg of Lamb, 108, 243

Mallard. *See under* Water Fowl
Marinated Duck Breasts, 182, 183, 243
Mascarpone Risotto, 86, 87
Mashed Potatoes with Fresh Basil, 62, 65, 242
Mayonaisse, homemade, 252
Meat grinders, 253

Menus
  For After a Day of Hunting, 237
  For People Who Have Never Eaten Game, 242
  For the Great Outdoors, 239
  For the Two of You, 244
  That Are Ooh La La, 240
  To Feed an Army or Hunting Party, 245
Meyer Lemon Sherbet, 50, 51, 96, 99, 238, 240
Minted Roast Duck with Potatoes, Carrots and Turnips, 169
Minted Roast Duck, Carrots and Turnips, 244
Mixed Bag, 201
Mixed Green Salad, 204, 241
Montgomery, Tom, 143
Mountain Goat
  Roast Leg of, 204
Mushrooms, dried wild, 249

O'Rourke, P.J., 81
Oils, good cooking, 249
Olive Oil and Salt Bread, 110, 112, 178, 180, 238, 239
Olives, 104, 105, 106, 114

Pans, small roasting, 253
Parchment paper, 253
Pasta
  homemade, 43
  machines, 254
Pasta with Chestnuts and Pignolis, 110, 111, 213, 214, 238, 242
Pasta with Fresh Chanterelles, 225, 227, 243
Pear Cake, 124, 126, 185, 187, 239, 244
Pen-raised, compared to wild, 256
Pepperidge Farms pastry sheets, 249
Pepperoni Bread, 54, 55, 193, 194, 244, 246
Persillade Potatoes, 52, 171, 172, 237, 238
Pheasant and Cabbage, 134, 246
Pheasant and Ruffed Grouse Sandwiches, 240
Pheasant in Wine, 120, 121, 245
Pheasant Salad, 130, 243
Pheasant Sandwich, 114, 115

Pheasant. *See under* Upland Birds
Pignolis and Raisin Cognac Stuffing, 196, 241
Pistachio Gelato, 225, 228, 243
Plain Roast Potatoes, 182, 243
Poached Pears, 74, 76, 152, 153, 242, 246
Poached Prunes and Apricots with Cognac and Cream, 213, 215, 240, 242
Portion control, 256
Potatoes and Porcini, 36, 37, 241
Potatoes Steamed with Sage, 166, 167, 243
Poultry shears, 252
Preserved Woodcock with Olives, 104, 241
Purée of Peas, 124, 125, 239

Quail. *See under* Upland Birds
Quail for the Campfire, 88, 240
Quail Soup, 110, 238
Quick Grilled Quail, 127, 240

Rabbit
  Braised, 216
  Salad, 219
Rabbit Salad, 219, 245
Raspberry Tart, 210, 212, 241
Red Pepper Salad, 238, 242
Red Peppers with Basil, 216, 217, 245
Reneson, Chet, 18
Reneson, Penny, 18
Rhubarb Tart, 71, 73, 117, 119, 241, 242
Rice, wild, 249
Roast Leg of Goat, 241
Roast Leg of Mountain Goat, 204
Roast Potatoes, 50, 57, 58, 136, 238, 240, 243, 244
Roast Potatoes with Rosemary, 57, 58, 176, 177, 238, 244
Roast Sheep, 213
Roast Wild Turkey, 117, 241
Roasted Duck, 166, 243
Roasted Sheep, 242
Ruffed Grouse Sandwich with Hazelnut Butter, 114

Saddle of Venison, 36, 50, 241
Salad with Hazelnut Dressing, 77, 244
Sandhill Crane. *See under* Upland Birds

Sausage, 225
Sautéed Bittergreens, 241
Sautéed Cherry Tomatoes, 139, 140, 185, 186, 244, 245
Sautéed Cucumbers, 216, 217, 245
Sautéed Green Beans and Cherry Tomatoes, 171, 238
Sautéed Mustard Greens, 196, 197
Sautéed Watercress, 50, 51, 127, 146, 147, 213, 214, 225, 227, 238, 240, 242, 243
SAVEUR, 20
Sea Duck. *See under* Water Fowl
Sea Duck Fricassee, 173, 174, 246
Sea Duck With Pancetta and Prosciutto, 238
Sheep
  Roast, 213
Shooting Sportsman, 20
Sliced Tomatoes with Basil, 74, 242, 245
Sliced Tomatoes with Fresh Basil
Smoked Goose in Cold Pasta Salad, 193, 246
Smoked Goose Salad, 188, 189, 241
Smokers, 254
Soup in a Pumpkin, 130, 131, 178, 179, 239, 243
Spinach and Bibb Lettuce Salad, 60, 239
Spitted Woodcock, 96, 97, 238
Stock, chicken, 251
Stock, veal, 64, 251
Strawberry huller, 253
Strawberry Ice, 39, 41, 60, 61, 238, 239
Strawberry Ice Cream, 39, 41, 238
Strawberry Tart, 120, 123, 182, 184, 243, 245
Stuffed Duck Breasts, 156
Stuffed Oranges, 56, 109
Stuffed Duck Breasts, 238
Stuffed Oranges, 54, 108, 243, 244
Sun-dried Tomato Bread, 104, 106, 188, 190, 191, 241
Sweet Potato Gratin, 69, 70, 237

Tangerine Sorbet, 100, 101, 166, 168, 243, 245
Tarte Tatin, 52, 53, 136, 138, 237, 238
Toll House Cookies, 102, 246
Tomatoes, sun-dried, 249

Upland Birds, 81
  Chukar
    Stuffed with Hazlenuts, 139
  Dove
    Fried, 102
    Salad, 100
  Grouse
    Pancetta, 93
    Sandwich with Hazelnut Butter, 114
  Pheasant
    and Cabbage, 134
    in Wine, 120
    Salad, 130
    Sandwich, 114
  Quail
    for the Campfire, 88
    Green Grape, 90
    Grilled, 124
    Quick Grilled, 127
    Soup, 110
  Sandhill Crane, 86
    Grilled Breast of, 86
  Wild Turkey
    Roast, 117
  Woodcock
    Armagnac on Garlic Toasts, 136
    Juniper Encrusted in Rosemary Cream Sauce, 108
    Preserved with Olives, 104
    Spitted, 96

Vanilla Ice Cream with Homemade Butterscotch Sauce, 62, 242
Vegetable Salad, 33, 35, 243
Venison
  Black Bean Chili, 28
  Burgers with Chateaubriand Butter, 33
  Calzone, 74
  Chops with Basil Cream, 77
  Chops with Blue Cheese and Caraway Seeds, 69
  Chops with Mustard Butter, 57
  Chops with Pignolis and Red Peppers, 54
  Grilled with Rosemary Butter, 67
  in Europe, 25
  in New Zealand, 25
  Native Americans and, 24
  Saddle of, 36
  Scallops, 52
  Steak with Red Wine, 71
  Steak with Wild Mushrooms, 60
  Steaks Marinated, 62
  Stew, 42
  Stew with Artichoke Hearts and Sun-dried Tomatoes, 46
  Strip Steaks, 39
  wild and farm-raised deer, differences between, 26
  with Port, 50
Venison Black Bean Chili, 28, 246
Venison Burgers with Chateaubriand Butter, 33, 34, 243
Venison Calzone, 74, 242
Venison Chops with Basil Cream, 77, 244
Venison Chops with Blue Cheese and Caraway Seeds, 69
Venison Chops with Mustard Butter, 57, 244
Venison Chops with Pignolis and Red Peppers, 54, 244
Venison Scallops, 52, 237
Venison Steak with Red Wine, 71, 242
Venison Steak with Wild Mushrooms, 60
Venison Steaks Marinated, 62, 63, 242
Venison Steaks with Wild Mushrooms, 239
Venison Stew, 42, 46, 47, 242, 246
Venison Stew with Artichoke Hearts and Sun-dried Tomatoes, 46, 47, 242
Venison Strip Steaks, 39, 238
Venison with Port, 50, 240

Wareham, Beth, 20
Water Fowl, 143
  Duck, any
    Grilled Breast of with Wild Mushrooms and Honey Mustard Sauce, 178
    Grilled Lemon, 185
    Grilled Marinated, 162
    Marinated Breasts, 182
    Minted Roast with Potatoes, Carrots and Turnips, 169
    Roasted, 166
    Roasted with Red Pepper Butter, 171
    Salad, 158

    Stuffed Breasts, 156
      with Ginger and Scallions, 146
      with Pancetta and Prosciutto, 176
      with Rosemary and Sage, 149
    Goose
      Christmas Anytime, 196
      in Cold Pasta Salad, 193
      Smoked Salad, 188
    Mallard
      Grilled Breast of, 154
    Sea Duck
      Fricassee, 173
      Grilled, 152
Waterman, Charley, 18
Waterman, Debie, 18
Waters, Alice, 25, 169, 170, 204, 206
White Bean Purée, 67, 68, 108, 109, 239,
    243
Wicker Bill, 81, 82, 85
Wild Rice with Walnuts, 245
Wild Turkey. *See under* Upland Birds
Woodcock. *See under* Upland Birds
Woodcock Armagnac on Garlic Toasts,
    136, 238

Zucchini Fans with Tomatoes, 102, 103,
    149, 151, 244, 246

About the author:

REBECCA GRAY has written nine books about food, including the best-selling *Eat Like a Wild Man*. She has been a contributing editor for *Sports Afield* and *Attaché* and written for *Field & Stream*, *SAVEUR*, *Town & Country*, *Playboy*, *Outside*, *Martha Stewart Living*, and many other publications. Most recently she served as an expert editor for the 75th anniversary edition of the *Joy of Cooking*. With her husband, Ed Gray, she founded *Gray's Sporting Journal*, the prestigious magazine about hunting and fishing. She lives in Lyme, New Hampshire.

www.ingramcontent.com/pod-product-compliance
Lightning Source LLC
Chambersburg PA
CBHW031240290426
44109CB00012B/369